BILLY CONNOLLY'S
WORLD TOUR OF AUSTRALIA

WORLD TOUR OF
AUSTRALIA

With photographs by Nobby Clark

BBC BOOKS

ACKNOWLEDGEMENTS

Firstly I'd like to thank the people of Australia for making me feel so welcome
and for making the tour such a memorable experience. Special acknowledgements
should go to Wendy Whiteley, Ken Done, Jimmy Pike, Peter Doyle and the Tiwi people
for all their help and cooperation in the making of the series.

As is usual in these situations, this tour would not have been possible without the assistance
of numerous people. Thanks in particular go to my promoters Kevin Ritchie and Harley Medcalf;
Janelle Mason and Peter Skillman of Shooting Star who supplied us with the crew and made all the
necessary arrangements; and John Wilson and Cheryl-Anne Whitlock, the researchers who
discovered so many wonderful places and people for me to visit.

Nobby Clark directed the whole proceedings with great patience and contributed many of
the photographs used in the book. Harry Mason, the production coordinator, took everything
in his stride whilst simultaneously talking into *two* mobile phones. Jim Walpole was our excellent
cameraman, aided and abetted by sound technician Ken Fryer and Brycen Horne, the camera
assistant. Thanks also to my trusty sound engineer Malcolm Kingsnorth, and to Terry Nicholson
for transporting the Harley trike across Australia with little or no sleep.

This book has primarily been compiled from the transcripts of the TV series along with
random extracts from my stage performance. Consequently I would very much like to thank
Claire Walsh for her invaluable help in compiling the book, ably assisted by Simon Prytherch,
Corrina Bryant and Pip Grant-Taylor. Finally, my gratitude to Martha Caute,
Linda Blakemore and Frank Phillips at BBC Books.

Billy Connolly

This book is published to accompany the television series
Billy Connolly's World Tour of Australia, produced by Sleepy Dumpling (Music) Ltd
for BBC Scotland and first broadcast in 1996

ISBN 0 563 38723 8
Billy Connolly has asserted his right to be identified as the author of this work,
in accordance with the Copyright Designs and Patents Act 1988 as amended from time to time
© Sleepy Dumpling (Music) Ltd 1996

Map by David Brown
Picture research by Frances Abraham

First published in 1996 by BBC Books, an imprint of BBC Worldwide Publishing,
BBC Worldwide Limited, Woodlands, 80 Wood Lane, London W12 OTT.
Reprinted 1996
Set in Janson and Franklin Gothic by BBC Books
Printed in Great Britain by Cambus Litho Ltd, East Kilbride
Bound by Hunter & Foulis Ltd, Edinburgh
Jacket printed by Lawrence Allen Ltd, Weston-super-Mare
Colour separations by Radstock Repro Ltd, Midsomer Norton

CONTENTS

Timor
Sea

Indian
Ocean

Great
Sandy Desert

Gibson Desert

WESTERN
AUSTRALIA

Great Vic
Deser

Pinnacles

Rottnest
Island

Perth

Sou

N
W E
S

0
0

800 km
500 ml

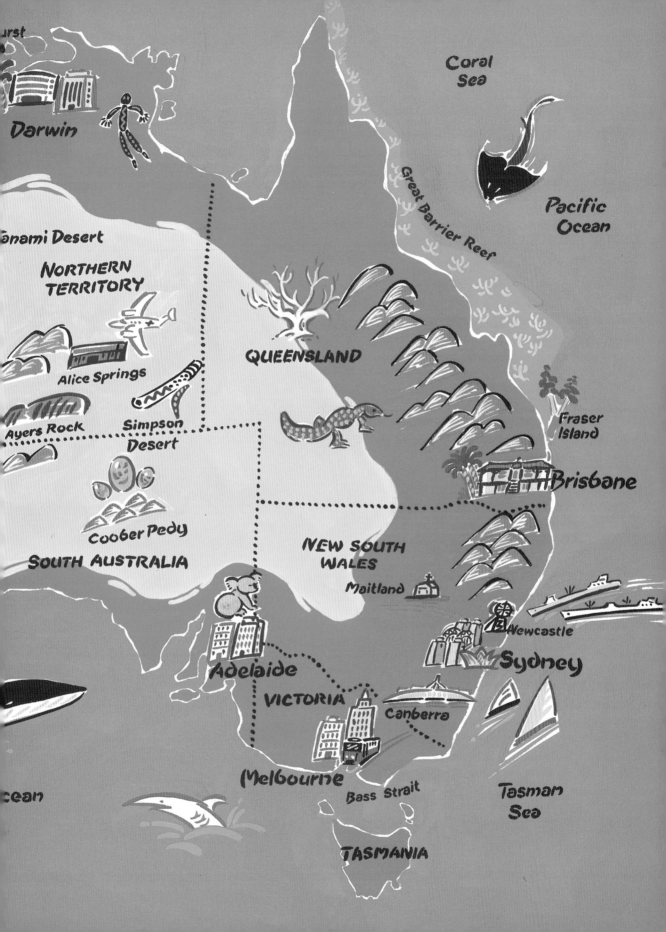

*This book is dedicated to the two Australians
who have had the most profound impact on my life:
my wife Pamela and the artist Brett Whiteley.*

INTRODUCTION

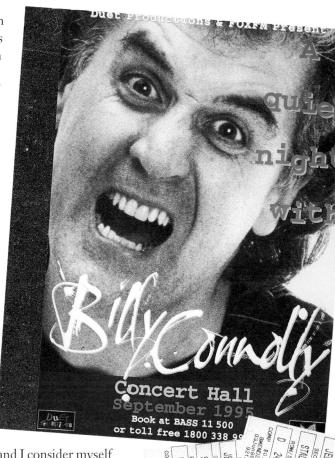

Welcome to Australia and my four-month tour. This book, like the television series *Billy Connolly's World Tour Of Australia*, is an account of my 1995 tour of Australia. I could have written a completely different kind of book – a travel guide – but I wanted to show you *my* Australia.

I have always liked touring here, it's a funny and enjoyable place. I want us to travel this extraordinary country together: first off, Sydney, then Canberra, Melbourne, Brisbane, Perth, Adelaide, Darwin and all sorts of weird places in between. I'm getting around by helicopter, seaplane, boat, four-wheel-drive and, best of all, a powerful, sexy Harley Davidson trike.

Australia is one of the most amazing and entertaining countries in the world. There's so much to see: from the wild and woolly countryside, rainforests and deserts, to the glistening modern cities.

I first came here nearly twenty years ago and I've lost count of how many times I've been back since. I like to return every couple of years or so, otherwise I begin to miss it. I have a great affection for Australia and I consider myself privileged to have witnessed its transformation over the years. During that time it has altered beyond belief. Australians have adopted a different attitude to their nationality. When I first started touring here, I recall that the majority of people I met seemed a bit jumpy and defensive about being Australian, but these days they are far more aware that this is a great country and one which they can call 'home' with pride. I hope that doesn't sound patronizing because this is a brilliant place with so much to offer anybody who comes here. There are very many 'Australian' virtues but for me, their greatest quality is optimism. The whole country has a youthful vitality which makes it an immensely exciting place.

I have derived enormous pleasure from my time in Oz, for which I would like to say thank you. *Billy Connolly's World Tour Of Australia* is my tribute to a wonderful people and a magical country.

SYDNEY

Sydney is Australia's 'Big Smoke' and the capital of New South Wales. It's a truly beautiful city with the harbour, Port Jackson, at its heart. You can't really claim to be in Sydney until you have the Harbour Bridge and the Opera House in your sights. I've been here many times but that first view of the harbour, bridge and Opera House still leaves me speechless.

A long-standing rivalry exists between the inhabitants of Sydney and Melbourne, as each considers their city to be the *true* capital of Australia. Canberra may lay claim to the title of Australia's *official* capital but you would be extremely hard-pushed to find a 'Sydney-sider' who would agree. Sydney is the birthplace of modern Australia – the landing point for the very first cargo of convicts transported here by the British over two hundred years ago.

On 29 April 1770 Captain James Cook sailed *The Endeavour* into the shelter of Botany Bay. Cook had been instructed by the British Admiralty to lead a scientific expedition to Tahiti. Also on board were scientists and a group of naturalists led by Joseph Banks, who named the harbour Botany Bay because of the many unfamiliar botanical specimens found ashore. Before departing, Cook named the newly-discovered land New South Wales and claimed the territory in the name of King George III and the British people.

Back home the powers-that-be were distinctly underwhelmed by Cook's discovery. They had been hoping that 'Terra Australis Incognita' would prove to be a bountiful land overflowing with gold, jewels, and exotic spices. Cook's report of a 'fine meadow' didn't quite tally with their expectations. New South Wales and Australia remained of little interest to the British until 1776 when the American War of Independence forced the government to look more favourably upon their new colony. The American Revolution had put an end to British use of the southern states of America as a dumping ground for convicts. The Government were faced with a seemingly insurmountable problem until Joseph Banks, who had accompanied Cook on his epic voyage, suggested that Botany Bay would be a perfect site for an alternative penal colony. Faced with overflowing prisons and the threat of social anarchy, the Home Secretary, Lord Sydney, ordered the British Admiralty to establish a colony in New South Wales. In 1787 the First Fleet, led by Captain Arthur Phillip, embarked on the 22 450-km journey and arrived, eight months and one week later, in Botany Bay.

Sydney Harbour with its two most famous landmarks, the Harbour Bridge and the Opera House. Breathtaking.

The greatest irony of all is that Captain Phillip was *deeply* unimpressed by what he found there. He had been expecting mighty rivers and lush green fields full of grazing cows. He was met instead by acres of sandy scrubland and a non-existent supply of fresh water. To make matters worse, the French explorer Comte de La Pérouse had been sighted in the area, possibly looking to conquer a new continent for the French. Captain Phillip decided to sail farther up the coast in search of more suitable territory. Twenty kilometres further on he chanced upon Port Jackson, 'the finest and most extensive harbour in the world', where, on 26 January 1788, he raised the British flag.

❝I'm getting around on a Harley Davidson trike. It's the most beautiful thing ever – a purple three-wheeler, a killer bike in the bad-boy position. It's not a peep-peep-excuse-me-bike but more a go-fuck-yourself one. I zoom past people in beige Nissans and they tell their children off for staring. "Don't look at him Dorothy! Next thing you know you'll be pregnant. Pregnant and taking drugs. He's a mad man. I saw him on the telly. His tits are pierced. He's probably got a big tattoo on his willy."❞

It is said that even the convicts cheered at the beautiful blue sea and golden beaches which greeted the fleet as it sailed into the harbour. A couple of Aborigines shouted 'Warra! Warra!' – Go away – but they were ignored. Within two years, over half of the Aborigines had been wiped out by the smallpox virus carried by the new arrivals.

In the meantime, the French set up camp briefly in Botany Bay, but La Pérouse was equally disenchanted with the locale and set off in search of new territories to conquer. How different it might have been if he had only dropped anchor twenty kilometres up the coast. The Australians might, to this day, be singing '*Dansant Mathilde*'.

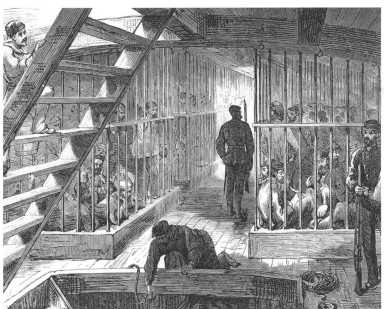

Above: The fleet of eleven small ships reached Botony Bay in 1788 after a journey of eight months.

Left: Imagine spending eight long months locked in a cell below decks. However primitive the conditions that they would face in the new penal colony, the convicts must have been glad to arrive.

The settlers clung for dear life to Sydney Cove, because that was where the colony's only fresh water supply for many years was to be found. Gradually their tents were replaced by brick and timber huts. Governor Phillip drew up plans for a carefully ordered town which the labouring convicts simply ignored – shortcuts became streets, and the resulting haphazard scheme is still evident today.

It took a Scotsman, naturally, to instil some order into the running of the colony and Governor Lachlan Macquarie ran it from 1810 to 1821. During his tenure he established the colony's own currency and the first bank. He appointed convicted forger Francis Greenway to be the chief architect of a programme of public works construction and town planning. Macquarie is also credited with naming the new colony Australia.

Transportation continued until 1868 by which time a staggering 160 000 convicts had been despatched. The population was further increased by the arrival of settlers, 70 000 of whom took advantage of the British Government's offer of assisted passage. On a visit to Sydney, Charles Darwin noted that transportation had failed as a system of reform but it had successfully turned vagabonds into active citizens, spawning a 'new and splendid country – a grand centre of civilization'.

The much-publicized discovery of gold by a prospector Edward Hammond Hargraves attracted a rush of new settlers to the colony and rapidly speeded up Australia's transition from a penal outpost to a proud nation. We should pity old Hargraves who discovered a tiny amount of gold and declared to a friend, 'This is a memorable day in the history of New South Wales. I shall be a baronet and you will be knighted and my old horse will be stuffed, put in a glass case, and sent to the British Museum.' He was right about New South Wales, but wrong in every other respect, passing an extremely uneventful life until his death in 1891.

In 1788, Sydney's population numbered 1030. Since the Second World War the city has experienced a mass migration of Italians, Greeks, Brits and Asians.

Today it is the continent's most populated city with 3.5 million inhabitants from every country on the planet. Transportation to Botany Bay was initially intended as a severe punishment for wrong-doers. Today, Sydney is known affectionately as 'the best address on earth'.

Raising the flag in Sydney Cove. The painting is called *The Founding of Australia* by Algernon Talmadge.

CIRCULAR QUAY WALK

Circular Quay, built on the site of Sydney Cove, is a great place for a wander.

The first settlers pitched camp here close to the fresh water supply and the city grew out from this point. These days, commuters and tourists gather here to take the ferries, and buskers and craftsmen provide many interesting diversions. If ever I have a spare half hour I can often be found strolling around the Quay. There are some smashing people around here.

There's a guy called India Bhauti and he just blows me away. I usually go and watch him in Melbourne where he plays outside the post office. I'm so pleased to have tracked him down in Sydney. He's brilliant. He wears a solar panel on his head which powers his instruments.

I met another entertainer, Johannes O'rinda, who whistles classical music – he's superb.

Below: Here I am listening to the incredible whistling man, Johannes O'rinda.

Opposite: The one and only India Bhauti. The strange-looking contraption on his head is a solar panel which powers his instruments.

SYDNEY OPERA HOUSE

The concept, design and the construction of the Sydney Opera House stand as an affirmation for twentieth–century man – that by his imagination and by his own hand he can shape the world to his own needs.

SIR OVE ARUP, 'Sydney Opera House'.

❛You have to open your mind to every new experience. This week I've been practising sneezing with my eyes open.❜

It is something of a miracle that the Opera House exists at all, as its construction was marred by a series of disasters culminating in the departure of the building's designer. The entire external structure was designed by Danish architect Jørn Utzon. The New South Wales government conducted a worldwide competition to design a complex of buildings to provide facilities for the musical and dramatic arts. The chosen site was Bennelong Point. The thirty-eight-year-old Utzon, a relatively unknown architect from Copenhagen, submitted the winning set of sketches – later described as 'a magnificent doodle'. The competition judges noted in their report that the 'drawings submitted were simple to the point of being diagrammatic', but they were swayed by the dramatic design which promised an opera house capable of becoming one of the world's greatest buildings.

Utzon's competition entry took full advantage of the dramatic mid-city, mid-harbour location, and his futuristic 'sails' were deemed to be a fitting symbol of Sydney's progress towards the twenty-first century. In 1957 he was appointed the architect of the project and finance was arranged through a special state-run lottery.

Construction began in 1959 and the attempts to transform Utzon's dream – or folly as it was later to be known – into a concrete and steel reality encountered the first of many structural and political problems. The shape and support of the 'billowing sails' – an essential component of the design – proved to be an almost insurmountable problem for the structural engineers. After four years' research Utzon altered his original design and the roofs were eventually pre-cast, greatly reducing the time and cost of their construction.

Can you see the wee dot on top of the Opera House roof? That's me.

The proposed completion date of 1963 passed as Utzon's team introduced numerous innovations on a trail-and-error basis. The series of lotteries were providing sufficient funding, but government alarm at spiralling costs and an unforeseeable completion date resulted in the appointment of a team of architects and the introduction of cost-cutting measures. This was the straw that broke Utzon's back and in 1966 he quit both project and country. His parting words to his successors were 'Tear it down'.

The first performance in the complex was a production of *War and Peace* on 28 September 1973, and the Opera House was officially opened by Queen Elizabeth on 20 October. It had originally been estimated that the project would cost $A7 million and construction would last five years. Incredibly, $A102 million was spent on the project over nineteen years, which was entirely paid off through the lottery by 1975.

To this day, Utzon refuses to return to Australia and view the completed building. By his own choice, he wasn't present at the opening ceremony and there isn't even a plaque dedicated to him in the entrance. There's a huge movement afoot here to rip out the inside of the Opera House and re-do it to Utzon's specifications. I'm very much in favour of this and I think it's a great move and would love to become involved. Ideally, everybody who has ever played the Opera House should get involved because it's one of the wonders of the world, like the Pyramids. It's probably the most famous manmade landmark on earth.

I thought I'd be able to sit astride it, but as you can see the roof doesn't really come to a point. What a view!

I'll never again look at the Opera House without thinking, 'I climbed up to the very highest peak and I stood right up there.' Astronauts must feel the same way when they look at the moon.

NIGHT WALK TO GIG

Another night, another dollar. Life is definitely sweet. I'm on my way to work, which tonight means the Sydney Opera House. It's strange, even now, to think that I'll be performing in the most spectacular-looking concert hall on the planet. I'm always a little nervous until I'm inside. From the outside it's unbelievably impressive. Inside it's just like anywhere else, when the lights go out.

I find that walking to the gig helps to ease any last minute nerves. It's something I try to do wherever possible. In Sydney it's a very pleasant stroll along Circular Quay to the show. Sydney has a unique way of celebrating literary heroes – they are given a plaque on the Writers' Walk on the Quay. For some reason, the plaque actually resembles an ornate manhole cover. I have no idea why this bizarre custom is observed nor what its origins are, but I think it's a lovely thing to do.

These are some of my favourite:

I love a sunburnt country,
A land of sweeping plains,
Of ragged mountain ranges,
Of droughts and flooding rains.
I love her far horizons,

❝Playing the Sydney Opera House is a bit like playing the Taj Mahal, it's a real-life legend. Isn't it the best-looking place you've ever seen? I love it. I always want to touch it and applaud it.❞

I love her jewel-sea,
Her beauty and her terror –
The wide brown land for me!
DOROTHEA MACKELLAR

Germaine Greer's has a lovely sentiment too:

Australia's my birthplace, but I cannot call it my own
as well as my native land, for I have no right to live there.
Until a treaty has been agreed with the original inhabitants,
I shall be homeless in the world.

I've always kidded this guy mercilessly about having a manhole
bearing his name.

In Sydney Harbour ... the yachts will be racing
on the crushed diamond water under a sky
the texture of powdered sapphires. It would be
churlish not to concede that the same abundance
of natural blessings which gave us the energy
to leave has every right to call us back.
CLIVE JAMES

'I've been reading about lesbianism and what lesbians like to do sexually. I think I might be one. We have similar tastes. Did you know that in Glasgow, cunnilingus is called "growling at the badger?"'

Clive's sentiment is one which crops up very often in Austalian literature, leaving and coming home are constant themes. Australians have a real pull to leave Asia where they feel isolated, and go to Europe where they come from spiritually, but I think it's becoming less important now as they identify themselves more and more with their country.

Barry Humphries' is real poetry:

> *I think that I could never spy*
> *A poem as lovely as a pie.*
> *A banquet in a single course,*
> *Blushing with rich tomato sauce.*

That's our Barry!

The guy who wrote 'Waltzing Matilda' and 'The Man From Snowy River' has one:

> *It's grand to be an unemployed*
> *And lie in the Domain*
> *And wake up every second day –*
> *And go to sleep again.*
> BANJO PATERSON

One of the things that has changed in the past twenty years is the way that the docks have become trendy harbour-front real estate. All the warehouses have been converted into galleries and restaurants – it's a worldwide phenomenon. As the docks become redundant, some property developer moves in and turns them into desirable residences.

It's a funny feeling walking up to this gig. Luckily the scary bit goes away quite quickly, because once you're under the first sail you could almost be in the boiler room of a hospital – it's completely unromantic and fairly unimpressive. Of course, that's exactly the way it should be. You can't stay impressed all night because if you're overcome with awe for the gig you would be unable to perform. Inside the Opera House it always looks and feels a little unfinished, like the set of some terrible Russian play. Until they do it the way that Utzon envisaged, it will always feel half-finished. However, the dressing room has a better view than any other dressing room anywhere in the world.

At night, the harbour area is almost as breathtaking. I find that walking to the gig takes away any last-minute nerves.

THE TANK STREAM

Below all the skyscrapers of Sydney's financial district runs the underground water source, the Tank Stream.

When Captain Arthur Phillip made his historic discovery of Port Jackson, the one feature of that area which was particularly important for the establishment of a settlement was the fresh water supply, which they named the Noble Stream. Later renamed the Tank Stream because of the three big holding tanks carved out by convicts to collect the water (you can still see the marks on the wall made by the convicts), for years it remained Sydney's only water source. There were very severe punishments for anybody found guilty of contaminating it – not unreasonable when you consider that this was the only source of fresh water. The penalty was to have your house pulled down and a fine of £5 for each offence, the money to be given to the local orphanage.

Well, after my intrepid climb to the top of the Opera House here I am doing the opposite – I'm underground and exploring the Tank Stream below the city streets.

By the 1820s the Tank Stream could no longer meet the burgeoning population's requirements and a tunnel was built to bring water in from the Lachlan Swamps. The Tank Stream became an open sewer and later in the century it was buried under tons of concrete to stop the spread of diseases.

It was also the scene of Sydney's first ever bank robbery. In 1828 Sydney had just two banks: the Bank of Australia, known as 'The Gentleman's bank' – mainly because rich merchants deposited their money there – and the Bank of New South Wales. A convict, Charlie Dingle, was working on a road gang when he realized that a drain running across the Tank Stream provided access to the foundations of the Bank of Australia. Charlie and four others, including a London safe-cracker called 'Sudden Solomon', hatched a cunning plan to break into the bank. Over several weekends they cut their way through a three-metre-thick wall, finally gaining entry on a Sunday. When bank staff arrived on Monday morning all that remained was a chest of silver plate. Charlie and his mates had successfully pulled it off.

❝Political correctness doesn't originate from politicians. It's a tool beloved of social workers. They are the living proof that a little learning is a dangerous thing. It's because of social workers that we have things in the street called "personhole covers".
It's not a personhole cover. It's a *manhole* cover. It covers a hole that a man goes down to delve around in the sewage. When women express an overwhelming desire to get up to their knees in shit, then they can change the name. Until then it's a *manhole* cover.❞

KEN DONE

Being in Sydney gives me the opportunity to catch up with my friend Ken Done. Ken is an extremely popular artist and designer, perhaps the best-known contemporary Australian artist. Ken's designs *are* Australia to much of the world. Two decades ago he was an art director working in advertising and then he did something which went against all common sense – he gave up his steady job, at the age of forty, to concentrate on painting and drawing.

What a welcome – Ken and Spot row out to meet me after I'd flown out to his home and studio by seaplane.

His work is instantly recognizable. Vivid colours and a simple, childlike style celebrate all things Australian: Sydney Harbour Bridge and the Opera House, sailboats and the beach, fish and flowers, kangaroos and koalas. Ken admits to a long-standing love affair with Australia, which he traces to early childhood. His father fought with the Australian forces in the Second World War and following his return home, the family moved to Maclean, a small town in New South Wales, where Ken recalls an idyllic childhood of 'long hot summers, cicadas, the beach, floods, gum trees, jacarandas, burning cane and Saturday afternoon at the pictures'.

Many of his paintings are inspired by the beach, harbour and garden, viewed from the studio at his harbour-side cottage on Chinamans Beach where he has lived for sixteen years with wife Judy and Spot, his dog. I went by seaplane to visit him – a brilliant way to travel as long as you don't think of Buddy Holly – and Ken, accompanied by Spot who goes everywhere he does, met me off the plane in his little boat and rowed me through the beautifully clear water to the shore. We made our way to The Cabin, a small white weatherboard house at the water's edge. The house is very modern and incorporates the studio where most of his work originates. The studio looks out on

to a fantastic view of the water which, along with the light, open rooms and the surrounding garden have provided subject matter for innumerable paintings and designs.

One of the most remarkable things about Sydney is that it is possible to lead a simple lifestyle, close to the beach and surrounded by the most beautiful clear water, while at the same time you are actually in the middle of a huge city. I have a theory that Sydney is actually what San Francisco thinks that it is. San Francisco promises a similar lifestyle but never quite delivers. Everything in Sydney exceeds expectations.

One of Spot the Dog's many appearances in Ken Done's paintings: *Walking the Dog*, painted in 1991.

Ken was born in Sydney in 1940. At the age of twenty he was appointed the art director of Australian Applied Advertising. Four years later, he left Sydney and travelled to New York and later went on to London where he worked very successfully in advertising. He and Judy married in London and settled in Chelsea during the swinging sixties, before returning to Australia in 1969.

As he grew up in a small country town, Ken loved to paint pictures, colour them in and show them to his parents and friends. As far as he's concerned that's exactly what he still does, but the paintings have become more complex, the colouring more detailed, and his friends and family are now a worldwide audience of many, many thousands.

I suppose you could say that he is extremely lucky to be able to do what he loves for a living but 'lucky' is a weird word. A lot of people miss the fact that 'lucky' people have in fact 'made it happen'. In the mid 1970s Ken was enjoying great success in his career: he had a harbour-side villa and the best of everything, but he felt something was missing.

In 1980 he made the momentous decision to support his family by painting and drawing. With hindsight, he agrees this was an incredible step to take: 'It's very easy to risk everything when you've got nothing. I reckon it's a bit more complex to risk everything when you've got everything.'

To promote the first solo exhibition of his paintings, Ken hung a silk-screened T-shirt from a tree accompanied by a sign: 'Sydney Harbour T-shirts $10 – please come inside.' The T-shirts sold like hot cakes and suddenly Ken had a whole new canvas for his work. He recalls that the popular success he has enjoyed sprang from the realization that people wanted to wear works of art. Today, his designs appear on swimwear, handbags, umbrellas, posters, jewellery, sunglasses, bed linen, towels, greeting cards and placemats.

The Japanese in particular are huge fans of Ken's work and admire the freshness and spontaneity evident in his paintings. The critics attribute his popularity to the fact that his work epitomizes 'Australianness' and points to the difference between the Australians

> ❝I passed a school – a very nice school – and some of the pupils ran out to have their T-shirts signed. There was one nice-looking wee guy, the kind of son you'd be well proud of, with bright eyes and curly hair. "Mr Connolly," he said, "I think you're a great comedian." "Well, thank you very much indeed," I replied. Then he said, "I loved that bit in your video when you say *Vagina* is a lovely word". I thought, "My God, what have I done?"❞

and the Japanese – Ken's work shows the Japanese what they are not and therefore enables them to see something else within themselves.

Ken feels that his work touches a chord in the Japanese psyche:

> *To many people my paintings would appear childlike, to the Japanese they appear sophisticated because it took me many years to develop the style.*

In his work, Ken uses one shade of blue a great deal and I have wanted to ask him about it for ages. It's exactly the same blue of as a flower called the Morning Glory – such a wonderful name for a flower. Ken often uses the same blue for borders and for water. He adds to the intensity of the colours in the same way that a musician might heighten the emotional sections of a particular piece of music.

Ken's experience of the world is determined by the emotions it excites in him and he tries to express those feelings through his work. This is not about logic but feeling: 'If something feels right I do it. My whole life has been like that, trusting in my emotions.'

Spot the dog makes frequent appearances in Ken's work as, being black and white, he goes with everything. When discussing *Walking the Dog* (illustrated on page 27), Ken points out that it's not an accurate representation of how he and Spot really look. The sky is never that red, the sea never quite that purple and the sand never black, yet it sums up Ken's feeling of walking at night after a hot day.

I talked to Ken about his work – I'm jealous that it is more permanent than mine. His will be there for posterity, I have to re-create mine every night on stage.

It could be said that Ken and I are both observers of the people around us. The similarities end there. I have to admit to an envy of artists whose work has a permanence. In ten years' time Ken can look at his paintings and recall the process of creating them. My work lasts for as long as I'm on stage. It all has to be re-created the next day. I need an audience for my work, while Ken tends to work alone with only Spot to give him the odd bark of approval. I want to make people laugh. Ken operates on the most simple level – he only desires that the person looking at his art should think, 'Oh yes, that's beautiful.'

If any of you are aspiring artists or if you would just like to be able to paint or draw, you could do a lot worse than to follow Ken's philosophy:

The more childlike my work, the better it is. I'd love to be able to draw as well as a five-year-old but I can't – that's a real challenge when you're fifty-five. I'm constantly in search of that freshness and simplicity. People tend to have it educated out of them. Those who don't know any better say, 'There are too many petals on that flower, it's wrong.' I think that's a shame. Clearly if I were a musician I would have to hit the right note every time but, that doesn't apply to art. So many people are disappointed because they believe they can't draw or paint – of course they can. It's just that they have an expectation that what they produce must be a realistic representation of what they're painting. I strongly believe people should draw and paint and forget about 'realism'. If you draw a cow, it doesn't necessarily need to look like a cow – just take the feeling of a cow, or flower or whatever you want, and use that as your inspiration. I paint what I feel.

Ken started out painting Australia as it looked to him. Now, everything has been turned upside-down and Australians have come to define themselves and their country in terms of the way they look to Ken. That's a wonderful thing for any one person to have achieved.

BOUNTY DAY TRIP

I'm aboard the reconstruction of Captain Bligh's ship, the *Bounty*, which was used in the film *The Bounty* with Mel Gibson and Anthony Hopkins. Normally it ferries tourists around the harbour, but not today. Today, I'm getting the full star treatment with a personal cruise.

Goat Island

Goat Island, a tiny speck in Sydney Harbour, was a self-contained penal colony. The punishments meted out at Goat Island were notoriously harsh, even by the standards of the day. One of the inmates was eighteen-year-old Glaswegian, Charlie Anderson, a former sailor who was transported for his involvement in a massive pub brawl. During his first year on the island he was such a nuisance that he is reputed to have received over 1500 lashes for bad behaviour and for his numerous attempts to escape. His escape plan was simple and pretty ineffective, consisting as it did of disastrous efforts to leap on to passing ships. Eventually the prison authorities tired of chasing after Anderson and sentenced him to be chained to a rock for two years.

Aboard the reconstruction of the *Bounty* and heading for Goat Island.

Above: Charlie Anderson's Couch. Charlie and I have something in common – a reputation for bad language. Right: Passing Fort Denison tower.

Sympathetic fellow prisoners carved a seat in the sandstone – now known as 'Charlie Anderson's Couch'. The eight-metre-long chain allowed Anderson to indulge in his favourite pastime – shouting and swearing at passing ships.

I had never heard of Charlie Anderson before this tour, but now he's my new hero and a pioneer of foul-mouthed Scotsmen. As you may know, I too have upset a few sensitive souls with my bad language and I've come up with a great tribute to Charlie. I'll make up some tapes featuring my best swearwords and rig up a speaker system to broadcast the abuse for the benefit of passing ships. What a fitting tribute that would be!

Pinchgut Island

During the Crimean War the British government fortified Pinchgut Island – so-called because convicts sent there were kept on starvation rations – because of fears of a Russian invasion. The tower of the fort – now known as Fort Denison – intended to house an enormous gun, was so badly designed that neither canon nor muskets could be fired from it. I love the way the human race is capable of such stupidity.

It takes a complete genius – probably a hippy – to design and build a fortress that has no defensive capability whatsoever. If it had been adequate to the task for which it was designed, it would just be another ugly reminder of man's lust for blood. But instead it serves absolutely no purpose, which in my eyes makes it quite a jolly little place.

Vaucluse

We also pass Vaucluse, a very posh area where my wife lived for a while. The original owner of Vaucluse was a wealthy but eccentric Irish baronet, Sir Henry Browne Hayes, who by all accounts was a bit of a lad. In 1801 Sir Henry had been sentenced to death for abducting a Quaker heiress, but was then transported to Sydney Cove. After he had served his sentence he settled in the elegant suburb of Vaucluse where he enjoyed a very pleasant lifestyle – with one exception. Sir Henry had an all-consuming fear of snakes and Australia is home to some truly fearsome specimens. In an inspired attempt to keep the snakes at bay, the baronet imported 300 barrels of Irish peat to be laid around the perimeter of the estate like a moat. As everyone knows, St Patrick banished the snakes from Ireland. Good old Henry knew that no snake would ever dare to cross a part of the old Holy Land. It's a bizarre notion but perhaps it had some foundation. Sir Henry later returned to Cork where he died in 1832. His motto was *Erin Go Bragh* – 'Ireland Forever'.

Doyle's on the Beach

What better way to round off the day than with a visit to the chip shop? This is not your average chippy, but one of Sydney's finest restaurants.

Doyle's on the Beach at Watson's Bay is my favourite restaurant in Sydney. The Doyle's story began with a tiny shop, on Watson's Bay promenade, and continues today with a chain of hugely successful restaurants famous for their superb locations.

Doyle's on the Beach is managed by Peter Doyle, the great-great-grandson of Grandmother and Grandfather Newton who opened a tiny little café in the late 1880s to cater for tourists visiting the bay. Grandfather Newton did the fishing and Grandma Newton would cook scones and fry fish and chips on a fuel stove at the back of the shop. The original café was pulled down in 1907 and the Ozone Café (later renamed Doyle's on the Beach) was built on the same spot.

Following the Second World War, the present owners Jack and Alice Doyle decided to re-open the business. They were initially refused a loan to cover the set-up costs

Below: Sitting with Peter Doyle in his famous restaurant. Opposite: How's this for a prime location? Doyle's on the Beach at Watson's Bay.

SEAFOOD RESTAURANT

DOYLE'S
EST. 1885

WATSONS BAY

Circular Quay 252 3400   Beach 337 2007   Wharf 337 1572

FULLY LICENSED

SYDNEY ROCK OYSTERS:

Native to Australia, Sydney Rock Oysters are found from Hervey Bay in Queensland to Wingen Inlet in Victoria. Rock oysters reach plate size in three years. They spawn in summer and spring and during this time they often taste a bit milky with a stronger flavour. Our oysters come predominantly from the Northern rivers of NSW.

SOUTHERN SCALLOPS:

Commonly known as Tasmanian Scallops they are found from Shark Bay, WA, to Tuncurry in NSW. Scallops take three years to reach plate size. Stocks are limited due to seasonal closures in different areas. Tasmania is at present the largest producer of southern scallops.

EASTERN KING PRAWNS:

Native to Australia, Eastern King Prawns are found from North Queensland to North Eastern Tasmania. More than 90% are caught north of the Tweed River. Prawns are a main source of food not only to man but to Dolphins, Seal, Rays and Flathead.

BARRAMUNDI:

Barramundi are widely distributed in coastal rivers and estuaries in the tropical and semi tropical region of Australia. They are a famed sportfish and superb eating. The flesh is moist, flavoursome and well textured.

SEAFOOD & ASPARAGUS CREPES

FRESHLY SHUCKED MANNING RIVER ROCK OYSTERS

SALAD OF RARE YELLOWFIN TUNA

OUR OWN FISHERMAN'S CHOWDER

EVANS HEAD MARINATED BABY OCTOPUS

SUSHI, SASHIMI & ROCK OYSTERS

QUEENSLAND KING PRAWN SALAD

SEARED TASMANIAN SCALLOPS

SMOKED TASMANIAN SALMON

OUR OWN JUMBO PRAWNS

PORT OF EDEN JOHN DORY FILLETS

WILD CAUGHT BARRAMUNDI FILLETS

BERMAGUI WHOLE SNAPPER

LIVE LOBSTERS FROM OUR TANK

Some of the things on Doyle's menu. Doesn't it just make your mouth water?

because the 'little, old café' was deemed to be a bad risk. Fortunately Alice's mum came to the rescue with the £60 needed to equip the restaurant and in 1948 Doyle's on the Beach reopened.

Today, the 'bad risk' café has become one of four restaurants frequented by international stars such as Frank Sinatra, Michael Jackson and Elizabeth Taylor. The Doyle's secret for success is perfect fresh fish, simply cooked and served – and plenty of it. The menu promises an extra portion of fish – free of charge – to anybody who is still hungry after their first serving.

Doyle's is still very much a family-run business. Alice Doyle has four sons, twenty grandchildren and ten great-grandchildren, many of whom are involved with the four restaurants. The success of Doyle's could put a lie to that old adage 'crime doesn't pay'. Peter Doyle jokes about returning to Britain, not to trace his own relatives but to thank those of the judge whose decision to send the first Doyle over made everything possible.

BRETT WHITELEY

Twice in my lifetime, a little bird has flown into my life and had a profound impact on my view of the world. On the first occasion I was quite young, maybe seven years of age, and on holiday with my family in Rothesay. I had been sent to buy bread and milk. On the way back a jackdaw landed on my head and said, 'Hello'. I thought I'd been sent for – I nearly had a coronary. I was a city boy from Glasgow and I had no idea that jackdaws could be taught to talk. Life had changed for ever.

The second time was when I met Brett Whiteley, who at that time was Australia's greatest living artist. When I first met him he was just a guy with curly hair and an enormous passion and lust for life. Whenever I think of him now I always see a little bird, and his ex-wife Wendy tells me that that's how he saw himself too. Brett had an incredible influence on me, both as a man and as an artist. He died of a heroin overdose in 1992, aged fifty-three. I miss him terribly.

Brett lived the way he painted – with passion. His life would probably make an unbelievable movie in which sex, drugs and rock and roll would feature heavily. But he was also plagued by a dark, threatening habit which eventually overwhelmed him.

At the age of eleven, Brett decided to become an artist. In 1955, when he was sixteen he wrote to his mother, Beryl, from boarding school and requested a second-hand easel. In his final months at school he sat at the back of the class, sketching anything which took his fancy. He had discovered his vocation.

The artist Brett Whiteley – I loved the man and his work. I miss him.

When his mother left Australia for an extended holiday in England, Brett threatened to leave school if she didn't return. He carried out his threat, walked out of school, burned his books and hung around with local meths drinkers for four days. Beryl's journey signalled the collapse of his parent's marriage.

Brett's father Clem remained supportive of his son's ambition, but urged him to find a skill to fall back on. In 1956, aged seventeen, Brett found a job with the advertising agency Lintas in Sydney. Largely

‘Brett Whiteley's not here any more and I feel really cheated that he died so young, because we'd only known each other for about four or five years. I loved him so much, he was such a funny guy. I used to do a routine about orgasms and that we are all only allocated 100 orgasms for our entire life. When you've used them up, that's it. So you have to use them sparingly, save them for special occasions. Brett gave me that idea. As a child, he was told not to masturbate because you only get 100 orgasms. On stage I say, I was so scared when I had the 101st.’

self-taught, Brett began to draw nudes at various night classes and sketch clubs. He also met Wendy Julius who was to become his lover, wife, mother of his child, friend, critic and combatant for thirty-two years.

In 1959 Brett was awarded a travelling scholarship, enabling him to travel to Italy and then on to London. Brett's arrival in London couldn't have happened at a better time. Australian art was receiving an inordinate amount of attention on an international level. Brett exploded on to the art scene in the midst of the swinging 60s when London was a playground for parties and miniskirts, Ravi Shankar and flower power, the Beatles and the Rolling Stones. The seven years spent in London were to have a great impact on his future work and life.

Brett's success was immediate and astounding. Three pieces of his work were shown in an exhibition of contemporary Australian painting in 1961 and they created a sensation. The Tate Gallery bought one and his reputation as an artist of international repute was established. In March 1962 he and Wendy married and spent six months in the south of France.

The Whiteleys' return to London was marked by Brett's increasing fascination with the female body. The result was the intimate 'Bathroom Series' which focused on the single figure – Wendy's naked torso in the bathroom. In 1963, news reached Brett of his father's death. His reaction to the bereavement was to bury himself further in his work. He had discovered a new and fascinating subject – violence and death. His particular interest centred on John Christie, a necrophile murderer who killed several women in London during the 1940s and 1950s. Christie posed as a doctor and lured

BRETT WHITELEY, *Lyrebird*, 1972-3.

his victims to his home with promises of a cure for all their ills. He then gassed them to death, had sex with the corpses and hid the bodies in the walls of his home. The 'Christie Series' was a sharp and explicit look at the evil side of human nature and sexuality.

In November 1967 Brett was awarded the Harkness Fellowship to study in the United States for two years. Brett, Wendy and daughter Arkie lived in the penthouse apartment of New York's notorious Chelsea Hotel which provided a stimulating but damaging atmosphere. The Whiteleys' relationship became complicated by new sexual and social freedoms, and both indulged in parties, extra-marital affairs and drugs.

Above: Brett Whiteley, *Lyrebird*, (1972-3). Birds were among Brett's favourite subjects.

Opposite page: Brett's picture of Rembrandt (1971-92), my all-time favourite amongst his work. The lovely big three-dimensional nose makes me jump up and down with glee.

The lovely Wendy Whiteley in Brett's studio.

'You pass this way but once. There's no such thing as normal. There's you and there's the rest. There's now and there's forever. Do as you damn well please or you could end up being a pot-bellied, hairless boring fart.'

Brett underwent a personal crisis with the increasing fragility of his marriage and a complete disillusionment with American society. He became absorbed with theories about the splintered self and psychosis. He had always been a hard drinker, but his drinking increased and became a real danger to his health. He began to lock himself into the studio and on two occasions Wendy took him to hospital with severe alcohol poisoning.

In July 1969, Brett flew to Fiji in search of a world far removed from the chaos and stress of life in New York. He was joined soon after by Wendy and Arkie. Those were happy days in paradise until a police raid on the family apartment discovered opium. The Whiteleys were thrown out of Fiji and returned, amidst huge scandal, to Sydney. They found a flat at Lavender Bay where Brett's fascination with addictive personalities and duality became evident from series of self-portraits.

One – a triptych called *Art, Life and the Other Thing* – is about the heroin which eventually killed him. At the time he painted it, Brett was thirty-nine and many of his friends did not expect him to reach forty. Alcohol had formed an important part of his life since he first left school. In London and New York during the 1960s he experimented a great deal with stimulants and hallucinogens. Then, in 1974, he and Wendy became serious heroin users. In contemporary interviews he was always forthright about his addiction and also his fear that without the drugs, his talent would just dry up.

During the late 1970s he and Wendy began to visit clinics to seek treatment for their addiction. It became evident that for Wendy to be really free from hers, Brett would also have to stop using heroin. He couldn't do it, and a separation in 1987 preceded their divorce. In 1992, Brett's body could cope no longer. He died alone in a motel room.

He is without a doubt one of Australia's most exceptional artists – and one of the most controversial. As well as his passion, Brett's other great quality was his ability to make people laugh. Critics had great difficulty with his humour. It's almost as if great artists with great passion are meant to sit amongst aspidistras and pontificate. Even his dress sense alarmed critics. He had a lovely collection of hats which he wore perched on his curls, and one critic was rotten enough to call him the 'Shirley Temple of the art world'.

I sent him John Kennedy Toole's novel *Confederacy Of Dunces* because it featured a quote from Swift: 'When true genius appears in the world you may know him by this sign, that the dunces are all in confederacy against him.' Never was it proved more true than when people were talking about Brett.

Brett's studio is a former T-shirt factory in Surry Hills. Outside the studio is the huge installation, *Almost Once*, which sums up Brett's life-long preoccupation with life and death.

I love it here because it resonates with Brett's incredible passion.

Greedily I await God. I'm an inferior race for all eternity.
To swim, to trample in the grass, to hunt, to bubble, to smoke, to drink
liquor as strong as boiling metal, like my dear ancestors around the fires.

If I had to nominate Brett's greatest quality, it would be his energy and the way he was able to harness it and channel it directly into his work. Brett didn't just paint things – he got right inside them. Galleries can be fairly stuffy but this one bursts with life, there's a huge three-dimensional quality about it, it's not just on the walls – it's in the air.

Brett certainly knew a thing or two about life and he lived it to the full. As he said, 'Life is brief, but my God, Thursday afternoons seem incredibly long.'

Wendy Whiteley is a walking work of art. She can be seen all over the gallery in various states of undress. I met up with the fully-clothed version at the studio. Wendy and Brett shared life, love, passion and the habit which was to lead to his destruction. Brett's life could have been different but perhaps his work might have suffered. Who really knows where life will lead us? Wendy knew Brett better than anybody in the world, and she has no doubt about what drove him on: 'Brett viewed contentment as a dangerous state – it was bovine. He needed to put his hand in the fire.'

As always, I spent time looking at Brett's powerful, passionate work and reminiscing about the great times we had together.

SYDNEY HARBOUR BRIDGE

Sydney Harbour Bridge – or 'The Old Coathanger', as it's known locally – is one of the modern wonders of the world, a truly spectacular sight. As you probably know I love engineering. All those rivets! All that steel! It's a fantastic tribute to human endeavour.

The Sydney Harbour Bridge was completed in 1932 and cost $A20 million which was only paid off in 1988. At the time of its completion it was the largest arch bridge in the world spanning over 500 metres and containing 52 000 tonnes of steel. The whole construction was prefabricated in Middlesborough, England, and shipped over for assembly. There is a wonderful story about the official opening of the bridge, which didn't go quite as planned. Premier Jack Lang, of New South Wales, was scheduled to cut the ribbon before an assembled crowd of Sydney residents, journalists and film crews. Without any warning a man on horseback charged out of the crowd raising a sword high above his head. The mysterious horseman was Irishman Captain Francis de Groot of the paramilitary New Guard. To the astonishment of the onlooking crowd he slashed the ribbon with a single stroke of his sword and announced that the bridge was open on behalf of 'the decent and loyal citizens of New South Wales'.

Naturally, De Groot was arrested and carted off to a psychiatric hospital where, I am delighted to say, he was found sane. The ribbon was re-tied and the official ceremony continued. De Groot was fined £2 for the ribbon and £4 for disturbing the peace before he was allowed to go on his merry way.

Above: Riding the Harley through the streets of Sydney.

Left: The Bridge – another climb ahead of me and the promise of 'the best view of a city, ever'.

My wife is Australian and she was consumed with envy when I told her I was going to the top of the Sydney Harbour Bridge. There is no better view of the city than from the very top of the bridge. There is a lift to the road level and then it's a long steep climb. It's hard work but the view is beyond belief. I'm not afraid of heights – in fact I love being up high and I couldn't wait to get to the top – but fear is the biggest danger in these situations. Remember that it's not the fall that gets you, it's the sudden stop.

Seen through the central girders, the bridge could be the world's biggest Meccano set. There are some truly incredible natural wonders in the world but creations like these just blow me sideways. I love what human beings are capable of.

Crocodile Dundee star Paul Hogan was a Sydney Harbour Bridge painter before he was discovered. Painting the bridge is a continuous job and a crew of a hundred men are employed to work all year long painting the bridge's span.

> ❝When I first became well-known, the reaction of some people was ridiculous. A crowd of autograph-hunters gathered round me in the street. There was one woman who kept saying. "Who is that man? Who? Well, I've never heard of him." She pressed closer and closer, before picking up a red and white cigarette packet from the gutter. I'll never forget it – it had a footprint on it – it was a dirty piece of crap. "You may as well sign that," she said. I signed it and gave it back, and she said, "That's going to my son in Australia."
>
> To this day, I have a private fantasy that her son is a rich Australian business tycoon, a big-shot with a house overlooking Sydney Harbour. I imagine him eating muesli in a Japanese dressing gown, opening a letter from his dear old Mum … and out falls that bloody fag packet.❞

A former welder's dream – being allowed to climb 'The Old Coathanger', the local name for Sydney Harbour Bridge.

Above: Clive James also climbed to the top of the bridge. He said it was hard on the knees and now I believe him.

Right: Wow, they were right. The view just blew me away.

Rehearsing doesn't work for me because comedy depends entirely on the laugh to get from one point to the next. If there's nobody there you're wasting your breath. I tried rehearsing – in the early days I tried in a mirror, but in a mirror you're looking the wrong way. I wasn't looking at the audience. I depend a great deal on the people. I don't know why nor do I know what triggered that dependence, but I absolutely need the audience. I rely completely on just walking on to the stage, feeling the atmosphere and getting on with it. I prefer to come out and do it to the public who bought the tickets, because that has its own atmosphere: there's a kind of bravery involved. It works, but it's also frustrating because if I do a funny walk and the audience laughs, then I don't know what they're laughing at because I've never seen it myself.

The way I work now is to have long periods off and then to work intensively. After a long period off, I've forgotten what I do for a living, what buttons to press to make it work. Some stuff I remember from before. I do take notes but they'll just say 'army' or 'ice skating', 'ballet dancing' or 'Scottish Nationalists'. Stuff like that. I'll go from there to a routine, which will grow as the tour goes on or sometimes it will shrink and new stuff will come in, and I'll keep repeating it and honing it down. I'm not really sure what I do. This is what I think I do.

I've always been convinced that the audience can spot the new stuff. They can tell when I'm ad-libbing. Sometimes I get so good at pretending to ad-lib that I might be able to pull the wool over their eyes, but I'm sure that when I'm being inventive they can spot it. They can tell because it has a different sound, there's a different atmosphere in the place – an atmosphere that I have become incredibly addicted to.

On most nights, if you get just a minute or two of ad-libbing, you're grateful it happened and you wonder where it came from – you never thought this thing in your life and, bang, you just start saying it, and people are laughing and you think, 'Thank you, whoever you are.'

NEWCASTLE

> *I became an Australian in Newcastle – I lost my Vegemite virginity there many years ago. It's remained with me ever since.*
>
> *I have it every day of my life, on my toast. It would be a bad day if I didn't have any Veggie.*
>
> *An American comedienne, who shall remain nameless, once said to me, "Eating Vegemite is like licking a cat's arse." I thought to myself, "How does she know?"*

Newcastle, or 'Steel City', is a great place. It is the second largest city in New South Wales, an industrial town where the coal mines and steelworks are the predominant sources of employment. Sydneysiders tend to display a slightly snobbish attitude towards the town and its inhabitants. I suppose that, by Australian standards, Newcastle is quite a rough place. However, Australia is paradise on earth, and what an Ozzie might constitute as 'rough' would seem pretty great to most people. The climate is warm, the beaches are superb and, it may be a cliché, but the people who live in this place work hard, play harder and are amongst the friendliest that I have ever met.

LES DARCY

I've always enjoyed boxing, but my affection for the sport puzzles me slightly as it goes against most of the things I believe in. While in Sydney, I visited the grave of Les Darcy, a great Australian sporting hero. Les Darcy, born in 1895, was the world middle-weight boxing champion when he was just eighteen years old. By the time he was twenty-one he had died, so legend has it, of a broken heart.

In the early twentieth century, boxing was probably Australia's most popular sport. By the time he reached the age of eighteen, Les was fighting in front of capacity crowds at the Sydney Stadium and was a popular working-class hero until the advent of the First World War.

In the first two years of the war 200 000 young Australian men volunteered to fight for King and Empire. Then, as the supply of volunteers dwindled, the Australian Prime Minister Billy Hughes became a vociferous advocate of conscription. Although he was under age, Les Darcy had stated his intention to join up, but his mother refused to sign the necessary papers and this took the matter out of his hands. Darcy immediately became a target for the pro-conscription lobby, and the subsequent controversy and a lack of realistic boxing opponents prompted him to board secretly a cargo steamer for the United States.

Darcy's arrival in New York in 1916 was hailed by the American sporting press, but back home, the Australian press branded him a 'shirker' and a coward. By the time these stories appeared, Darcy was in Memphis, Tennessee, preparing for an exhibition fight, when suddenly he fell inexplicably ill.

The fight promoter released a statement to the press claiming that Darcy was suffering from flu but that he would be well again in time for his scheduled fight. In fact, Darcy had a serious blood infection, probably contracted as a result of dental treatment to correct a previous boxing injury. Only five months after his arrival in the US, Les Darcy died.

His body was taken back to Sydney where a crowd of 100 000 was waiting. His coffin was put on open display and 300 000 people are said to have filed past it to pay their respects. Les Darcy was finally buried in his home town of Maitland. To the disgust of Darcy's critics, the state railway ran extra trainloads of mourners from Sydney, Newcastle and Cessnock and the funeral cortège was said to be over 5 kilometres long. Before Darcy's body was lowered into the ground, there was a simple and moving eulogy: 'We are proud of Darcy and never have we been prouder of him than today, for we are able to give his calumniators the lie by virtue of this great demonstration. Before the grave closes over him, in his name we can forgive his enemies.'

My daughter Daisy once told her friends that her father was a 'comedium'. She got it bang on. It's like I'm talking and someone else is giving me the ideas. I've never thought this thing in my life and suddenly I'm hyper. Maybe it's adrenaline, maybe just general nerves and excitement. All my senses are right on the edge and this thought comes out of my mouth and it works. Sometimes I do feel like a comedium – it's a wonderful feeling. A weird mixture of nerves, odd noises and relaxation.

A lot of my energy comes from anger – anger and coffee.
The only time I ever drink coffee is before I go on stage.
Just before, I have a really strong coffee and I get very jumpy
and speedy. I go on stage flying, like the cops are at my back
and I'm overwhelmed by anger. But then I'm angry anyway.
I'm angry at the world, I'm angry at right-wing politics,
and I'm angry at the state of the place. I get angry about
litter, I get angry about graffiti, I get angry at politicians,
I get angry at selfishness and I get angry at pretentiousness,
and I just love attacking it all.

One of the great joys of life is to be given a microphone
and a spotlight and to be allowed to say anything you damn
well please. You've no idea how brilliant that is. There's no
drug on earth to equal it. I can attack anything. I can attack
the Pope. I attack politicians that are supposed to represent
working people and don't. I can attack the government, ice skaters,
a bar of chocolate that irritates me – anyone and anything, the
world is my oyster. Sometimes I regret it and sometimes I have
to pay for it, but it's such fun. I cannot exaggerate enough the
overwhelming rush of adrenaline I get when I'm attacking
somebody, kicking a big fat arse that really deserves it.
There is no equal to it on the planet, and that's what
keeps me going.

CANBERRA

This is Canberra – Australia's official capital city. Ask any British schoolchild to name the capital of Australia and I guarantee that the answer will be either Sydney or Melbourne. The entire reason for Canberra's existence was as an attempt to clarify that confusion. In 1901, when the separate colonies were federated and became states, the government decided to build a national capital. A site was chosen at a diplomatic distance between the rival cities and given the name Canberra, supposedly after an Aboriginal word meaning 'meeting place'.

Incredibly, the Government held an *inter*national competition to design the capital city. The winner was an American – Walter Burley Griffin – who can be held single-handedly responsible for the city plan. If there's any justice at all, I'm sure he's roasting in hell. This is probably the most inert, sterile town on earth.

Griffin's original plan was for a garden city, structured around five main centres. Construction began in 1913 but the onslaught of the First World War disrupted work, and Parliament House wasn't opened until nearly ten years after that. The Depression and the Second World War virtually halted further development.

At that point, it should have seemed obvious that somebody was trying to tell them something. The most sensible idea would have been to abandon the grand plan and go home. However, with typical persistence the Australians kept at it and in 1958 they created the National Capital Development Commission. Between 1960 and 1967 the population of 50 000 doubled.

In 1963, the Molonglo River was damned to form the artificial lake at the centre of the Canberra design – Lake Burley Griffin. To me, this manmade lake epitomizes everything that is wrong with 'new towns'. Towns have traditionally grown up around natural resources such as rivers or mines where industries can establish themselves. But Canberra is built around an artificial lake.

If there is one good thing to be said about Canberra, it is that it is an outstanding example of what happens when politicians are allowed to create towns. Real towns grow up gradually and are in tune with the needs of their inhabitants. Canberra has developed as a result of a political idea and, in keeping with those origins, it is all style and no substance. This is a place for politicians to show off and to wander around looking important. Canberra is really an Antipodean Brussels,

Arriving in style outside the New Parliament House in Canberra.

stuffed full of pompous politicians, dreary diplomats and catatonic civil servants. Besides being the capital of Australia, I would hazard a guess that it's also the bullshit capital of the Antipodes.

There have been attempts to make the city more exciting by the developments of all those institutions associated with capitals – a National Gallery, the National Botanic Gardens, the National Museum of Australia, and even a National Aquarium. None of them can detract from Canberra's in-built, over-designed lack of character.

Canberra is home to about sixty diplomatic embassies. The city is full of grand driveways and terrible glorious sculpture. It's very similar to Russia. The whole place has a quite Teutonic air, with lots of pillars and columns – it's the kind of place the Nazis would have been proud of. The streets are eerily quiet, with no people anywhere to be seen apart from the odd security guard. Call me a paranoid old person but it always feels as if people are peering at you from behind their curtains.

The original Parliament House opened in 1927. Ironically, the 'meeting place' was to become the site of a confrontation between the white settlers and the indigenous Aborigines. Two Aboriginal men, Jimmy Clemence and John Noble – who called themselves King Billy and Marvellous – staged the first official Aboriginal protest in front of the newly-opened building, and quite rightly so. Their cause was the recognition of the Aboriginal people as a distinct race, entitled to basic human rights. They stood their ground for as long as possible but were eventually chased off and run out of town.

As late as 1972 the Government passed legislation stating that the Aborigines had no rights to any of the country's natural resources. The Aborigines were 'allowed' to remain on Australian land but the law declared that they owned nothing. On Anzac Day in 1972 a group of outraged Aborigines established a protest in the grounds of Old Parliament House, dubbed the Tent Embassy. The protest camp became a focus for Aborigine activism and witnessed the first public exhibition of a new Aborigine flag. The flag, designed by Harold

> Politicians suck. For a long time I have believed that the desire to be a politician should prohibit you from ever becoming one. The lust for power is a dangerous thing. There's one very simple rule to adhere to when dealing with politicians – if you wouldn't talk to them in a bar, then don't vote for them.

> Isn't it refreshing to see that politicians dance as badly as medical students?

Previous pages: Tight-arsed and super-structured, the city is a place for politicians to show off. It's the bullshit capital of the Antipodes.

Opposite: The present-day Aboriginal Tent Embassy.

Thomas, featured three strong colours – black for the people, red for the land, and a circle of yellow representing the sun. The Tent Embassy remained in place for six months until a hastily-approved bye-law prohibiting camping on public land put an end to the protest.

The fight for the recognition of Aboriginal rights continues to this day. A new embassy has been established since my last visit here. The Aboriginal Tent Embassy was set up in 1992 to safeguard the sovereignty of the Aboriginal people and to protest that Australia wasn't discovered but invaded by white settlers. And they are quite right too.

To celebrate the bi-centenary, it was decided to build a brand new state parliament. The result was a staggering building costing an even more staggering $A1.2 billion. The opening ceremony in 1988 was held amidst great pomp and ceremony and huge fanfares . In this case, deservedly so, because it really is the most extraordinary-looking place. I was actually in Australia at the time and I recall there was a great deal of fuss about the huge metal sputnik affair on the roof. I personally like it. It's a modern building and the mast is in keeping with the futuristic design.

The thing that most fascinates me about Parliament House is the fact that there is a huge lawn that goes right over the top of the building. So amazingly, in Canberra, it's possible to walk all over the government. They're all underneath there, puffing out their chests and congratulating themselves on their self importance and all the while, the voters can trample over them. Most of

‘Don't vote. It only encourages the bastards. Be an anarchist. Are you telling me that politicians know something we don't know? Keating and Howard, they don't know *anything*. They all love Margaret Thatcher because she's the biggest shit of them all. They all admire her, whatever their politics, because she did what they'd like to do. Fuck up the whole country.’

the time, the hill is redundant but I've come up with a great use for it. Whenever politicians are caught out lying, they should be made to roly-poly all the way down the hill. Naturally, since politicians can barely open their mouths without telling a fib, this lawn should rapidly become the busiest and most entertaining part of Canberra.

In addition to the canvas Tent Embassy, Canberra is home to embassies and high commissions in all manner of designs. Some are spectacularly beautiful, some have quiet good taste, others show great ethnic features typical of the home country, and the rest are all in remarkably bad taste. The British Embassy falls into its very own category: stultifyingly boring. It's like a Russian Civil Servants' Bridge Club.

On the other end of the scale is the Chinese Embassy which wins my prize for the most impressive building in Canberra. It's enormous – almost the size of an entire Chinese village. There is a funny tale about this Embassy. Apparently the Australians were caught out in a hugely bungled attempt to bug the place, much to their embarrassment, and the Chinese discovered microphones secreted all over the place.

I love the Papua New Guinea Embassy which is based on a spirit-house in the country's Sepik region. The main part of the building is in the style of a Taberan which is the traditional place for storing sacred treasures and for meetings of the elders. Most of the embassies have signs pasted all over the place saying things like 'GET OUT OR THE SOLDIERS WILL SHOOT YOU!' This embassy just has a nice polite sign saying 'VISITORS WELCOME'. It's a lovely, dignified place.

The Indonesian Embassy is also rather beautiful. It has a modern glass façade and a great Hindu temple with sculptures all over the place. The notable thing about this embassy is that it is ambassador-less. There was an ambassador but it emerged that he was the General responsible for the massacres in East Timor. The Australian public was outraged and he fled the country in fear for his life.

The French Embassy used to occupy a nice quiet corner in Canberra. It was all very reserved and sophisticated, with the smell of croissants wafting over the lawn whilst you imagined the ambassador drinking his wine to the strains of Charles Aznavour. But now the place

Top: The frontage of the huge Chinese Embassy.

Above: Some of the few signs of life in the area – protests outside the French Embassy.

is jumping since the French started setting off nuclear bombs in the Pacific. Directly opposite the Embassy is a permanent camp of protesters urging people to vote for a nuclear-free Pacific. The placards are all terribly polite: 'WE ENTREAT YOU, RESTRAIN YOUR RUTHLESS WARRIOR LEADERS.' I must say, I'm on their side.

Canberra tries hard to project an image of itself as a fun, carefree city but the sad truth is it's just plain dull. I personally think it's crap, but the people who live here love it. I have relatives who live here and they don't have any problem with the place – but it's not my cup of tea.

Rodin sculptures in the Sculpture Garden of the National Gallery, Canberra.

All my life I've been clumsy. Those ashtrays on aeroplane armrests have always popped out into my hand and spilled ash all over the aisle. Other people open them perfectly well. There's a U-shaped piece of metal which is supposed to put your cigarette out but it would never do it to mine. I would scrub around it and take the head off and shut the lid, and for hours smoke would come trailing out. I'd cover it with my hand, I'd put my jacket over it for fear of setting the whole plane on fire. That kind of thing has happened to me all my life and I discovered that talking about it made other people laugh.

I seem to have this ability to see absurdity in the most ordinary things. I see great danger in the things that are supposed to help you. I have the kind of mind that always imagines something awful happening and I'll take it to a silly degree. I love the safety instructions on aeroplanes. In your heart you know that if you come out of the sky it's over. Your cushion's not going to help you. Your inflatable life jacket's not going to help you. And a whistle in the middle of the Atlantic Ocean is about as much use to you as an ear on your forehead.

I've always seen the terrible absurdity of life.
It doesn't frighten me at all.
It does make me roar with laughter.

MELBOURNE

Melbourne is a magical city. Set upon the Yarra River, it has a far more European atmosphere than any other Australian city I've ever visited. At the same time it is home to such truly Australian exports as *Neighbours*, Fosters lager, Dame Edna Everage and, my favourite, Vegemite.

You can't go much farther Down Under than this – only Tasmania is closer to 'the end of the earth'. Melbourne was founded in 1835 by Batman – not the caped crusader, but John Batman, a lecherous alcoholic who died in the advanced stages of syphilis. Batman's most notable contribution to Australian history was to utter the immortal words 'This will be a place for a village', and for making an illegal treaty with the local Aborigines to exchange 592 000 acres (240 000 hectares) of land for 30 tomahawks, 40 blankets, 200 handkerchiefs and a quantity of flour.

Melbourne really came into its own when, in 1851, gold was discovered at nearby Ballarat. Gold fever hit Victoria in a big way and thousands of migrants invaded the state in search of the buried treasure. It is perhaps no coincidence that medical records of the time note that more people were diagnosed insane in Melbourne than in any other city in the world. This was a time of amazing prosperity for the area and Melbourne soon became known as 'the working man's paradise'.

The good times couldn't last indefinitely and the 1890s witnessed the most severe economic depression in Australian history. However, many of the foundations had already been laid for Melbourne to become the great city it is today.

Sydneysiders often complain that Melbourne is sedate and dull, but I have to disagree – Australia's second-largest city is not dull, it has a relaxed, cosmopolitan culture.

Melbourne is often viewed as the seat of the Australian Establishment and that's why it has a reputation as a conservative and stodgy place. Many of Australia's premiers, bankers, stockbrokers and lawyers are the product of the city's élite private schools and colleges. Think of every old cliché about English public schools – clock towers and cricket pitches, blazers and head boys – they all apply in Melbourne, where there are long waiting lists for entry to many of these establishments.

Magical Melbourne – relaxed, laid-back ... whatever you want to call it – but never dull. And they make Vegemite here. I love it, it's brilliant!

Melbourne has been described as the 'Athens of Australia', and certainly I don't think I've ever seen more publicly displayed art anywhere else apart from Rome. It overspills from the galleries out on to the streets and into the parks. There are sculptures and paintings all over the city and I love the way they are often in places where you least expect them.

The city is connected by a tram network which offers a laid-back view of the urban landscape. I haven't been on a tram since I was a wee boy. They're brilliant as they go at the proper speed so that you can see the world, they're ecologically sound and make the city look so good.

> ❝I'm a devoted *Neighbours* watcher and I'm in love with Annalise. I'm getting old and I now realize what a dirty old man is. Don't women just look amazing these days? I think there should be a day when you're *allowed* to touch them – Old Man's Day. Just one day, when we'd be allowed one feel an hour. You'd get a cup of tea and a biscuit to bring you round afterwards.❞

Melbourne has been much maligned over the years. Ava Gardner, here to film *On the Beach*, commented that it was the ideal setting for a film about the end of the world. Dame Edna, Melbourne housewife extraordinaire, claimed it was the only place on earth where people debated the possibility of death before life. However, Melbourne's 3 million residents can't all be wrong. The truth is that Melbourne is a cosmopolitan city which owes much of its character to its inhabitants, amongst whom, at one time or another, have been Germaine Greer Barry Humphries, and Rupert Murdoch. Melbourne was always a traditional landing place for immigrants, particularly for the Scottish, Irish and British. In the past fifty years, there has been a huge influx of Europeans and Asians in search of a better life. The resulting multicultural society is vibrant and multi-textured, offering new culinary and cultural experiences which have greatly enriched Melbourne life.

Residents of Melbourne have a standing joke about the weather: if you don't like it, just wait a minute. It's completely unpredictable and four seasons in one day isn't unusual. No matter the weather, Melbournians' enjoyment of sporting fixtures is unsurpassed even by Ozzie standards. Melbourne is home to two of Australia's greatest sporting passions: Aussie Rules Football and the Melbourne Cup, the famous horse race first run in 1861.

Driving in downtown Melbourne. I recommend the city's tram network if you want to explore – you can see everything at a relaxed pace.

SCULPTURE WALK

It's not difficult to discover great art in Melbourne – just take a look around you. The Victoria Arts Centre is slap bang in the centre of town and I think that's a very good thing. Approximately half a mile along are all the shops and cafés. The sculptures are so accessible. There's one which looks like sections of some enormous pipe. Children sit on it, they play and have picnics by it and they bring the whole thing to life.

I was raised a Catholic, and my father once told me about a local Irish priest . He was the talk of the town because he put on quite a show. He would just lose it completely, get very carried away, a specialist. He'd rant and rave, 'You shall go to hell, and you will boil in the fires of hell! You'll be standing in hell, up to your knees in the filth, the filth of hell and the rats of hell and the beetles, and the worms will be crawling up your legs. You'll cry and whine and beg for mercy, "We didn't know it would be like this!" you'll say, "We didn't know." The filth will climb higher up your body and the flames will be licking at your feet. The beasts of hell will eat you alive, and you'll be crying, "Oh God, we didn't know," and God will say, "Well, you fucking know now."

I love modern sculpture – I have an affection for it that has taken me completely by surprise. I never wanted to like modern art, I just found that I did. I also like ballet, for the same reason. My daughter forced me to take her to the ballet one night and I immediately fell in love with it. It's like being given a present when you discover something which you'd intended to dislike on principle, creeps up on you and puts you under its spell.

The Messenger (illustrated overleaf) is the work of a guy called Geoffrey Bartlett. I won't pretend that I understand its meaning but I just like it. It's a welding thing and as you know I like anything to do with welding. At night it looks truly spectacular because it's lit by street lamps and spotlights which produce three different shadows along the wall, and it looks absolutely brilliant.

It's a funny thing, but Australians are becoming increasingly like Middle Eastern people. They spend a great deal of time just sitting and looking – Arabs do it all the time. It's living sculpture. I think it's a very good thing to learn. When you're feeling a wee bit jaded – have a seat. Just sit down – it doesn't matter where you are.

The Victoria Arts Centre. This guy's a great favourite of mine. I've tried for years to get a picture of him looking at a helicopter or plane but I've never managed it.

Above: This amazing sculpture of three narrow-shouldered guys going home to the suburbs of an evening, had rubbish piled up in front of it because of the garbage men's strike when I was there. I thought they looked horrified.

Right: The sculpture is Geoffrey Bartlett's *The Messenger*. The guys are two of the film crew.

Far right: A great favourite of mine is called *The Lost Purse*. I love it because it's a happy and accessible sculpture, but a lost purse is kind of a sad thing, isn't it?

MORNINGTON PENINSULA

Mornington Peninsula is a boot-shaped land-mass enclosing half of Port Phillip Bay, just a short drive from Melbourne.

In 1802 Governor Philip Gidley King, of Sydney, prompted by fears of French attempts to claim the territory on the newly-discovered Bass Strait, ordered that a settlement be established at Mornington Peninsula. One of the settlement party – a convict named William Buckley – escaped and was 'adopted' by a group of Aborigines. Thirty-one years later, when John Batman, arrived he discovered a wild white man – Buckley – who had to be virtually re-taught his native language.

Harold Holt

In 1967 Mornington Peninsula became headline news. Australia's Prime Minister Harold Holt disappeared from here under mysterious circumstances. Holt was reputed to be what the Australians call a larrikin – a bit of a lad. He'd come here for a picnic, a swim, a few beers with some friends. They went for a swim and after they had dried off and lazed around for a bit, he decided to go back for another swim alone. Harold Holt, the prime minister of Australia, then walked down to the sea, dived in and was never seen again.

Mornington Peninsula is a beautiful area not far from Melbourne. In 1967 Prime Minister Harold Holt (above) disappeared here while swimming.

The people of Australia have been talking about his disappearance ever since. Many books have been written about it and theories proposed. Was he dragged out by the tide and drowned? Perhaps he was eaten by a shark? Did he meet a Russian submarine out there? Or was there some other reason that we dare not consider? We will probably never know.

Even to this day Australians have an expression: 'Doing the Harold', which means to shoot through and make a hasty exit. People say it's rhyming slang for 'Harold Holt' – to bolt.

When I heard about Harold Holt's death, I thought, "Now that's a country that knows how to treat its politicians properly." Poor old Harold – eaten by a shark. We asked for one for Thatcher for years, but it wasn't forth-coming.

Newspapers of 1967 and 1970 show the headlines breaking the news of Harold Holt's disappearance and the tragedy of the Westgate Bridge collapse.

WESTGATE BRIDGE

On the outskirts of Melbourne is the Westgate Bridge. The bridge is a famous landmark with an unbelievable view from the top.

On 15 October 1970 the partly-constructed bridge collapsed and thirty-five men plunged to their deaths in the Yarra River. This was a real tragedy for Melbourne, not least because the bridge represented everything about the new Melbourne and the city's growth. The men who lost their lives were iron-workers, carpenters, fitters and a boilermaker. I'm a boilermaker myself and it breaks my heart to think of the world being a boilerman short.

The Westgate Bridge disaster: a 120-metre section of the bridge weighing 2000 tonnes crashed to the ground from a height of 47 metres.

PECIAL EDITION

(Classified 63 0301)

SEA

ails

ly

Fitwear
SOCKS & KNITWEAR

THE AGE

Melbourne, Friday, October 16, 1970

6c   60 0421

Sir Henry Bolte promises Royal Commission into disaster

32 men die—how many mo

Search of ruin resumes at first light

The West Gate bridge disaster death toll stands at 32. Nobody knows how

OLD MELBOURNE GAOL

Old Melbourne Gaol, opened in 1845, is now a pretty macabre museum in the city centre. It's a terrible place, and well worth a visit if, like myself, you have an interest in the seedier side of life. The first thing that strikes me, whenever I enter a prison, is how anybody could come there more than once. My personal theory is that it's the magnetic odour of early-morning urine that has them coming back for more.

Throughout the years 104 hangings took place at the gaol. There are hundreds of fascinating stories about this place. Here are just a few of my personal favourites.

George Melville was hanged here in 1853 for his involvement in a gold robbery. After his death, the prison authorities released Melville's body to his grieving widow. Mrs Melville had his body delivered to her oyster shop in Melbourne, where it was seated in a chair and decorated with flowers. According to the newspapers of the time she then did a brisk trade, regaling her customers with tales of police brutality and corruption. The prison authorities subsequently decreed that the bodies of all executed convicts must be buried within the prison grounds.

The death mask of gold robber George Melville, hanged in Melbourne Gaol in 1853.

In 1890 Frances Knorr was bumped in here for infanticide. Her husband had been imprisoned in the same gaol three years earlier for the heinous and shocking crime of – gasp, horror – selling furniture on hire purchase. With her husband and breadwinner in the slammer she was completely broke and took up what was then called 'baby farming' – child minding – to earn a living. However, when two or three of her charges went missing and their bodies were found in various gardens, Frances Knorr was sent to Melbourne Gaol and sentenced to hang. She was an incredibly popular local figure and the people of Melbourne demonstrated to prevent her execution. Even the hangman's wife threatened to leave him if he carried out the execution, but two days before the hanging, he committed suicide.

'Laughing Eddie Lionsky', an American pilot who was stationed in Melbourne during the Second World War, was charged with

The interior of Old Melbourne Gaol and probably its most famous exhibit, the armour worn by the notorious outlaw Ned Kelly.

strangling three women. At the trial he pleaded insanity which was rejected, despite his continuous laughter throughout the court case. He kept on smiling and laughing all the way to the gallows and was still chuckling to himself as he dropped through the trap door.

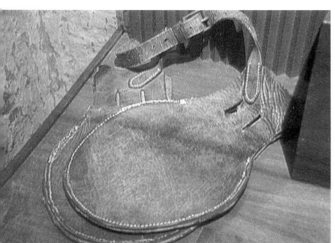

At Melbourne Gaol, I came across the most devilish, most cunning, most awful instrument of torture – a pair of big, circular leather gloves. Their sole purpose is the prevention of self-abuse among prisoners. They are anti-masturbation gloves and it makes me shudder just to look at them.

In the eighteenth-century the science of phrenology was very popular, much as astrology is today. Phrenologists believed that they could gauge human personality and predict behaviour traits by identifying bumps on the skull. It has since been discredited but, at the time, people would take their bumps to be felt up by the local phrenologist. For example, if you had a lump in the area just above the ear that was taken as an indication of destructive tendencies, as it had been observed that the skulls of violent men were raised in that area.

After an execution, a death mask was made of the convict's head and phrenologists were invited along for a prod. One of them examined Ned Kelly's mask and came to the staggeringly perceptive conclusion that he was a man destined to lead a life of crime. What a genius!

The life of a prisoner has certainly changed over the years. Let me give you a couple of examples. John Perry was sent down here for assault in 1881. He was originally given eighteen months but the sentence was extended for tobacco possession and disobedience.

In 1889 Robert Maloney came here for burglary but his sentence was increased as punishment for whistling in his cell at 5.30 a.m.

Top: Anti-masturbation gloves – the ultimate torture instrument.

Above: The flogging machine.

When I first saw the flogging machine I thought it could be a number of things: an easel for an artist who doubles as a billiards player, or perhaps an ironing board for the horizontally challenged, or maybe a surfboard for an agoraphobic. And no, it's not for rent. The prisoner would be strapped to it and then flogged liberally about the back and buttocks. The flogging was usually carried out by another prisoner. One of the inmates – Michael Gaiety – was an expert flogger. As a reward he was given permission to marry a female prisoner and they were allocated a double cell.

Housed in the prison is a display of instruments used to torture prisoners: a kidney belt, a cat o'nine tails, and single and multiple canes. A collar was thoughtfully provided to prevent the neck from being damaged. The funny thing is that I've seen most of these things openly on sale in Melbourne's sex shops.

'The one advantage masturbation has over sex is that you don't have to look your best.'

'Sex is a very nice thing. But I remember my first sexual experience as a very frightening experience – it was dark and I was alone.'

'You know, I've always been pro-masturbation. It's the only exercise some of us get. I have to do it to get my heart started of a morning.'

This is Ned Kelly,
Australia's Robin Hood.

'Why do they
call it the bush?
Surely it should be
plural – the bushes,
for God's sake.
Imagine walking
across country and
suddenly you come
across *the* bush.
"Oh this must be
the bush" – with
4 million kangaroos
hiding behind it.'

BUSHRANGERS

Ned Kelly is perhaps the most famous bushranger of all, but these colonial highwaymen were a prevalent feature of desolate bush roads. The bushrangers were often 'bolters' – runaway convicts – whose speciality was the removal of cash and jewellery from hapless travellers. They were protected by some of the rural inhabitants who saw many of the outlaws as rebels fighting against the English authorities. One of them, 'Gentleman Matt' Cash, was the ancestor of another famous Australian – Wimbledon tennis champion Pat Cash.

Ned Kelly was born in 1854 in Northern Victoria. In 1877 he shot a policeman in the wrist and fled to the bush with his brother and two friends to begin life as an outlaw. A year later Ned was tracked down by a party of four policemen – he killed three of them and stepped into Australian folklore as a latter-day Robin Hood. Ned considered himself a freedom fighter campaigning against the oppression of English overlords. They, in turn, saw him as a hardened, homicidal maniac.

The one characteristic which differentiated Ned Kelly from other bushrangers was his sense of style. He was nothing if not dramatic and thumbed his nose at merely robbing coaches and travellers like the other bushrangers. Instead, Ned and his gang preferred to hold up entire towns, cutting off the telegraph and robbing the bank before fleeing into the bush.

In June 1880, the Kelly gang discovered that they had been betrayed by an old friend and that a trainload of police was on its way to their hideout. They came out fighting and ripped up the tracks on which the police train was due to arrive, captured the town of Glenrowan in Victoria, and held all the inhabitants hostage in the pub. Ned was wounded during the ensuing shoot-out and attempted to escape in his suit of home-made armour. The armour, fashioned from the mouldboards of a plough share, weighed 44 kilos.

Unfortunately, he stumbled into a police ambush. The armour deflected numerous police bullets leaving him very badly bruised about the body, until it occurred to the police to shoot at his legs. He was hanged in Melbourne Gaol on 11 November 1880.

Ned Kelly was my type of guy. After a bank raid in 1879 he wrote a wonderful letter, which included the following words:

I have been wronged and my mother and four or five men lagged innocent and it is my brothers and sisters and my mother who had no alternative only to put up with the brutal and cowardly conduct of a parcel of big, ugly, fat-necked, wombat-headed, big-bellied, magpie-legged, narrow-hipped, splay-footed sons of Irish bailiffs of English landlords.

Before he fell through the little trap-door to his death, his last words were 'Such is life'. I couldn't have put it better myself.

A newspaper illustration showing the last moments of Ned's life. He was hanged in Melbourne Gaol in 1880.

THE WILLIAM RICKETTS SANCTUARY

God-love, pulsating in a rhythm that moves and swerves through all life.
To understand your highest self you must live in that rhythm.
WILLIAM RICKETTS

On the slopes of Mount Dandenong, two hours from Melbourne, lies one of the most impressive places I've ever visited in Australia. It's a rain forest created by a most remarkable man. William Ricketts was a visionary who believed Australia wouldn't be able to survive on the tired old values of Europe. His work in this sanctuary is a testament to that belief and is a symbolic embrace of the values of native Australia. It's an extraordinary shrine to an extraordinary man.

Despite having had no formal artistic training, Ricketts created an elaborate panorama of sculptures populated with intricate representations of himself, his family and friends. This was literally his life's work and by anybody's standards, it's totally remarkable.

In 1935 Ricketts and his mother came here to live in a tiny cottage in the forest. William's father was a violent alcoholic who terrorized his wife and son until they could take no more and they escaped to the sanctuary of this place. They were very happy in this idyllic setting and the result was this tremendous outpouring of creativity. William was a sensitive soul and once free of the violent and restrictive influence of his father he concentrated on the creation of a new world in which the Aboriginal and Western cultures merged.

One of William's dreams was that one day there would be a school, an educational system, where Aboriginal children would learn about their own culture – a dream well worth pursuing. One of the sculptures, which he called *My Country*, is an expression of that wish: a portrayal of Ricketts' spiritual self embracing a group of Aboriginal children.

The whole area is endowed with a remarkable atmosphere. You lean on something, thinking it's a banister and discover it's a carving of an Aboriginal child's head. Incidentally he didn't use a generic Aboriginal head, every single head in the park was modelled from a real and individual person.

But for me the *pièce de résistance* is a beautiful plaque. It encapsulates Ricketts' discovery of his spiritual awareness through his life here with the Aborigines: 'This my life has a wholeness of meaning because of my innermost experience. I have come face to face with those beautiful life principles Jesus spoke of and which are the light of the whole world.'

‘There's a bunch of mountains here called the Dandenongs. What a brilliant name. Hanging's too good for them – they need a good kick in the Dandenongs.’

Opposite: This is a sort of self-portrait – William Ricketts' vision of himself in the Aboriginal Dreamtime – half man, half kangaroo.

Away from the road you come to the first big piece of William's work. The theme which recurs again and again throughout the forest is the Aboriginal symbol of concentric circles representing the soul as the font of spiritual energy. The flow of the water symbolizes the

outpouring of spiritual energy, rippling outwards through the concentric circles. The whole sculpture flows upwards to the creative energy of the hands. The creative spirit flows up through this amazing tribal elder, a personal friend of the artist, right into the trees and beyond. It really is a lovely and enriching sight.

Another favourite of mine is William Ricketts as he envisaged himself in his spiritual state (illustrated on page 84). This is a representation of the Aboriginal 'Dreamtime' when the earth was peopled by spirits who were at once animal and human. They were enormous and created everything, mountain ranges, huge caves, rivers and seas. William's top half is in his human guise but the lower part of his body is that of a kangaroo. In his hand he cradles a koala with a tiny possum sitting on its shoulder. It's a wonderful representation of the Western world merging with the Aboriginal world.

A lot of the pieces in the forest have an almost lofty, spiritual feel about them. In *Betrayed* he didn't beat around the bush. Oh no, in this piece he really gets down to the

Top: A beautiful carving of a child's head. None of the work here is generic, all the models were real, individual people.

Above: *Betrayed:* the symbolism here doesn't leave much to the imagination.

meat-and-two-veg of life in Australia. He depicts the 'gun brute of Australia' – a man with grasping clawing feet, a crown of bullets and shells, carrying two guns. The 'gun brute' represents the government. Ricketts hated the fact that the government taxed sporting rifles and so benefited from the slaughter of Australian wildlife. The clawed feet represent greed: for instance the destruction of forests for gain. At the base lie all the dead animals, the extinct flora and fauna. To one side is a crucified Aborigine in agony – just like Jesus. On the other side is William, also on a cross but his expression is serene. Ricketts believed that he could help by standing and fighting for the rights of the Aboriginal people and to right the wrongs which have been done. A small plaque expresses that sentiment: 'My spiritual self with Aborigine is not meant to express agony, betrayed.' It's a wonderful thing that screeches volumes. If it was airy-fairy and hippy it would be a wee bit suspect, but this is so powerful. I love it.

I find it quite incredible that nobody has capitalized on the sanctuary. One of the extraordinary things about the William Ricketts sanctuary is that there isn't a theme park or anything remotely like that. To get here, you leave the normal world, with all its cars and highways and enter this environment built by a single man. It's so peaceful and brilliant – if you ever get the chance you must go. I can't begin to adequately describe it but there's a plaque here, made by the man himself which explains what its about: 'In all this sanctuary there's one theme only, expressing reverence for life in the new world environment.'

The shape of one piece – a large oval – symbolizes the entrance to the womb. When you walk through it you enter the Great Mother's womb. When you leave you should be a different person, you should have experienced a kind of rebirth. It's all about

One of William Ricketts' extraordinary sculptures.

rites of passage. John Morrison, the caretaker here, told me about an Italian rite in which the parents of a newly-born baby split a sapling tree and pass the baby through it, bring it back and then seal it all up again. In the modern world, it's almost as if we're experiencing a panic as we seek out rites of passage that have some meaning. People are being pierced and scarred and tattooed, inventing new religions and new ways to worship in old religions, in an attempt to find out who we are and where we came from. This seems to be the obvious answer and it makes great sense to me: just step into a new world and step out a new man.

There is one sculpture here which sums the whole place up. It's called *Earthly Mother* and it depicts the mother figure with all her children. She's the giver of life and she's feeding the whole world. It has an important message: look after nature and nature will look after you.

New venues, new engagements make me nervous.
As does going from a big venue to a little one, going to places
where I'm really well-known, going to places I'm completely
unknown. But it helps the performance. The worst thing is to go
on feeling completely confident. I hate that feeling. The actor
Russell Hunter told me, 'If you're not nervous, drink a lot
of water. You'll need to pee and it'll make you jumpy
and apprehensive.' And that works perfectly. I need to be
jumpy to get the best out of myself.

Bill Kerr once told me that he spoke to Tony Hancock
just after he'd done the Blood Donor sketch. Hancock was
unbelievably depressed. Kerr had just said to him, 'For God's sake,
that was stunning. What's wrong with you?' And Hancock replied,
'How am I going to follow that?' I understand his panic perfectly –
you're up against yourself every night. When you do really well,
everybody says 'Well done', and you have your dinner and go
to bed and think, 'Oh God, I have to do it again tomorrow night',
and the next night and the next. The most terrifying thing for a
comedian is knowing you have to do it again tomorrow.

The main aim is to get into a position where you can do
it to order. You can do it if you think you've got the flu
coming on, you can do it if the weather's lousy and you've just
had rotten news from home. You have to be able to do it in any
circumstances: that's the biggest challenge of comedy.

ADELAIDE

Adelaide, in South Australia, was never a convict settlement. Free settlers were lured here with the promise of small plots of land and civil and religious liberty. The first settlers arrived in 1836. In 1841 the state had gone bankrupt but was bailed out by British Government funds until the discovery of huge copper reserves ensured its prosperity.

Adelaide is South Australia's principal city, situated approximately one third of the way from Sydney on the extreme east coast to Perth on the far west. It's a nice old-fashioned kind of town, comparatively free of the pollution, street crime and traffic jams which plague other Australian cities. Adelaide is an extremely pretty place; it's also the centre of a huge farming area. The city centre, on the banks of the Torrens River, is surrounded by green parks and rolling hills. Even in the height of the arid summer, some ingenious irrigation systems ensure that the parkland remains lush and green, which is quite a feat when you realize that Adelaide lies on the very doorstep of some of the harshest, driest land in the world.

A British engineer, Colonel William Light, was responsible for the establishment of the city of Adelaide in its present site on the western side of the hills. Light based the city plans on the design of Catania, a town in Sicily, and the Mediterranean influence remains a very strong aspect of the city.

It's a really relaxing place to visit – a very easy-going place, and it has a nudist beach – what more could anyone want?

Adelaide is also known as the 'city of churches'. In the early days, all people who settled here were granted complete religious freedom – a major attraction during the nineteenth century. Inevitably the different churches of their various religions sprang up all over the place. Adelaide was said to be full of 'wowsers' – the Australian term for puritans.

❝I was in a hotel once and I was surprised and shocked to see a mirror above my bed. "Oh God! What's expected of me now?" It's very rare to see yourself lying down, isn't it? Your face sort of all spreads out. I looked up and I thought "Oh Jesus, I've turned into my mother." And I've never understood why anybody would want to be shagging away and look up and see this big, white, spotty arse …❞

❝Talking about hotels – don't ever have sex on nylon sheets. It can't be done. It's the weirdest experience in the world. Your pubic hair stands on end and sparks fly out of your armpits.❞

The pretty city of Adelaide is surrounded by hills and amazingly, its parks manage to stay green even in the hottest season.

GLIDER

One of my lifetime's ambitions has been to fly in a glider. In Australia I was able to fulfil that ambition. When I was younger some of the guys I knew – the posh ones – were in the ATC (Air Training Corps). They used to go gliding and I was consumed with envy.

I met the pilot, Bob, and was a little surprised to learn there were no parachutes. Bob assured me that he had every intention of coming back, but a parachute would have been nice anyway.

Bob told me to get straight into the glider, which took me by surprise. In Britain I'd have had to fill in a load of forms in triplicate, but here it's, 'Hi, Billy, I'm Bob. Get in.'

You have to take advantage of the opportunities life throws at you. Gliding will remain with me as one of the most exhilarating and memorable things I've ever done – backwards, forwards, upside-down, loop the loop at 1400 metres. It was amazing. Unbelievable. After we'd landed, I got out of the glider and wasn't sure whether I was glad to be down, or glad I went up. It was simply stunning, terrifying!

Opposite and below: I look pretty confident here in the pre-take-off pictures, don't I?

Above: Ten minutes later, when the earth was above me and the sky was under my feet.

93

MY PIE FLOATER

I do like to partake of local delicacies on my travels. You can tell a lot about a nation by its food. America brought us hamburgers, Scotland gave you haggis, the Welsh love leek soup and the Irish adore mashed potatoes mixed up with spring onions. Here in Adelaide I discovered a real Southern Australian speciality – the pie floater. We're talking proper food here – man's food, none of your Continental rubbish. Pie floaters are sold from a road-side kiosk, like a burger van, and the basic components of this culinary delight are a meat or chicken pie, and pea soup. Barbecue sauce is optional but highly recommended.

The important thing is to make sure the pie is completely covered in thick, green pea soup – really smother it. Add the sauce or vinegar if you like and enjoy. It's real satisfying food, brilliant. The singer Joe Cocker always has shepherd's pie delivered to his dressing room at gigs – everywhere the world over except for here in Adelaide. Then he has a pie floater sent in from this very kiosk.

They hold competitions here for eating the most floaters – the record is nine in three and a half hours.

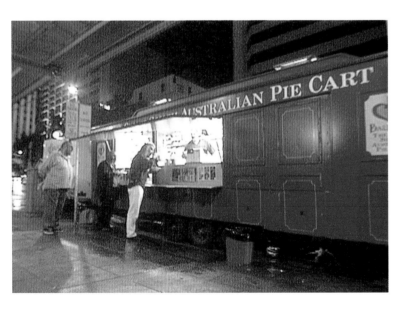

Above: Here I am buying my pie floater. If you try one, remember it comes highly recommended – by me and Joe Cocker.

Right: The Festival Theatre complex and some unusual sculpture.

I mostly relate to vaudeville comedians. The people who inspired me to be a comedian were Chick Murray, Max Wall, Frankie Howard and the Scottish ones like Jack Radcliff, Stanley Baxter and Jimmy Logan, especially Jimmy Logan because he was funny in my accent. When we listened to the radio and watched TV it was all Charlie Chester, Jimmy Wheeler and Dave King. They were all very, very good, but they were English and it was foreign to me. Then I'd go to the theatre and Jimmy Logan would be there being extremely funny, in my accent about things I knew about – about coalmen and streets that I knew and about things I saw every day of my life. It had a profound effect on me and I decided then that I would like to be a comedian. It sounded like a very normal, strong and good job – to go and be one of those guys.

I come strolling on, almost like a boxer. Comedians and boxers are very alike. A boxer is alone out there except for his opponent. I don't have an opponent and I'm not in conflict with the audience, but something has to happen. With a boxer, one of them has to win. With a comedian, if the audience laughs you've done well, if they don't laugh you didn't do it. So I come on a bit like a boxer and I stride around the stage. Ideas are going round in my head. I put out my feelers, I see what they like, what they laugh at, what they find funny, see how far I can push the boat out. Once it settles, I'm away and the act achieves a certain rhythm. I can do it for hours and hours. Usually I look at my watch and I've done two, or maybe two and a half hours. So I say, 'Well, let's wind it down,' but sometimes it takes me three-quarters of an hour to wind down. It's a jolly thing. I feel the audience, they feel me, we like each other but I have to perform. It's boxing. It's a game.

Empty stages are kind of strange. If you ever get the opportunity, walk on to a stage after the show has been on and the performers and the audience have left. It's wonderful because you can still feel the people in the room. Some theatres have a wonderful atmosphere because for years people have been coming in and having a great time. Churches have a certain atmosphere in much the same way. You can feel all those people and all those years: people who met there and then got married. The theatre has an atmosphere of its own – a sort of shabby, chic atmosphere.

PERTH

Western Australia covers a huge area of land – it's larger than Texas and Alaska combined, yet a mere 1.5 million people live here. The state is also home to 40 000 Aborigines, many of whom live in abject poverty in the remote Outback.

In 1827 the British despatched Captain James Stirling to explore the Swan River as a potential site for white settlement. The black swan, after which the river is named, has become the state symbol of Western Australia. Stirling was enraptured by a spot where the river widens, 16 kilometres upstream from the Indian Ocean, and sent back glowing reports. The first settlers arrived there in 1829 and a gold rush in the 1890s saw the population rocket from 3000 to 30 000 by the turn of the century.

Perth is so isolated from the rest of the continent that it's known as Cinderella City – it's actually nearer to Singapore than to Sydney. It's an isolated city but it's a good city. It's also called the 'City of Light' because Perth, discovering that it was below the first ever orbit of the earth, switched on all the city lights so that the astronaut John Glenn would be aware people were still at home.

We have Perth to thank for the Pavlova – that delicious concoction of meringue and fruit and cream. In the 1920s the Russian ballerina Anna Pavlova visited Perth and she stayed in a hotel called the Esplanade. The hotel chef created the Pavlova dessert as a tribute to her.

There's a road in Perth lined with gum trees, each of which is dedicated to a soldier who died in war. It really is very moving as most of them were only in their twenties. What a waste. There's one lovely quotation from a mother: 'I don't know where my son's body is, but his soul is here.'

Left: Perth is known as Cinderella City.

Above right: Taking the bike through the avenue of memorial trees, each one dedicated to a soldier killed in the Second World War.

‘Australian cities are all miles away from each other. Perth is miles away from *everywhere*. It's closer to the moon than it is to Melbourne. I love Perth – anywhere that has a grassy beach gets my vote. I hate sand, it's horrible stuff – it gets everywhere. I've hated it all my life. I've been married twice and I've had two lots of children – two lots of sand. Yes, you know how it goes … "Let's bury Daddy!"’

Motoring around Perth on the old trike.

Above: Cute, isn't he? How could they confuse him with a rat? It's a quokka.

Below: I meet one up close.

ROTTNEST ISLAND

Nineteen kilometres from the coast of Perth is Rottnest Island. Rottnest is Dutch for Rat's Nest and it was given this charming name by an early Dutch explorer who mistook the island's hordes of tiny marsupials – quokkas – for rats. Quokkas are actually delightful creatures – a lot like little wallabies, with rattish tails and a pouch in front.

The Aborigines call the island Wagemup which means 'land across the sea'. It was made into an Aboriginal penal colony in the 1830s which was not closed until 1903 – Western Australia doesn't have a great history when it comes to the Aborigines.

Motor vehicles aren't allowed on the island and it's a fantastic place for cyclists – if you survive the boat trip. I've always said, if you're going to vomit, make sure you do it somewhere spectacular.

Having been relieved of my breakfast, I set off in search of quokkas. There's an Australian singer called Barry Crocker who sings the *Neighbours* theme tune. I vote that all quokkas should be called Barry after him as a salute.

Tea-trees

I remember the days when the only use for the tea-tree was as a winning word in Scrabble. These days tea-tree oil is so trendy. It's the latest magic potion – a cure-all for anything from acne to arthritis. People rub it into their nooks and crannies, drink it in tisanes, clear their sinuses with it – anything and everything you can think of. I've only ever seen it in little bottles before, but the tea-tree grows in abundance on Rottnest Island.

Hairy-Nosed Wombats

Finding a quokka, made me think of some of Australia's other furry animals. The hairy-nosed wombat is fantastic, one of my favourites. I have to admit to a long-standing fascination with the creature ever since I heard Pam Ayres talk about it – I couldn't believe there was really an animal of that name. Languishing in Newcastle, England, is a very special example of the species. In 1790 a British explorer discovered one in Tasmania and took it back home to Britain. After the animal died, it was sent to be stuffed and put on exhibition. Unfortunately, the taxidermist had never seen a wombat before so he stuffed it standing upright like a kangaroo. So for many years, the British people thought that there was a funny fat kangaroo with an even funnier name. It really resembles a huge overgrown mouse and it moves around on all fours. It's the most pleasant-looking animal.

The hairy-nosed wombat has a pouch, the same as a kangaroo except that it's round the other way, with the entrance near the hind legs. This is because it digs with its front legs and would fill the old-style pocket with earth – and the wee baby wombat would say, Give me a break here! So how long did it take evolution to do that? I lie awake thinking about it.

These creatures are prodigious diggers – much to the annoyance of gardeners. They actually live in the holes that they dig out, but they are also infamous for the way in which they will tunnel into someone's garden – but then instead of going back through the same tunnel, they dig another. As these animals aren't small you can envisage the size of the tunnel.

The hairy-nosed wombat is now an endangered species. Recently they found out that there were less than a hundred in Queensland – so now it is officially protected.

Kangaroos

We're often hearing about indigenous animals that have only been saved from extinction by the narrowest of margins. It's comforting to know that Australia's most famous marsupial, the kangaroo, has defied current trends and there are now more kangaroos on the continent than there where when the first Europeans arrived in the 1800s, despite the legal culling of over 3 million of the creatures every year. Kangaroo meat is an increasingly popular item on the menus of Australian restaurants.

Koala Bears

The cuddly koala bear is just about everybody's favourite animal. It sits up there in the trees, the hippy of the animal kingdom, munching away on the green stuff, looking kind of stoned. Even close up and in the flesh it looks like a living teddy bear.

A typical hairy-nosed wombat? The British thought so for years due to a taxidermist's mistake!

❛Our nose is badly designed – the snot falls out. If there is going to be stuff in your nose, it shouldn't be runny and able to dribble out. Really, our nose should be on the other way up – but then, when you sneezed, your hair would get two side partings and your eyes'd be full of snot. Also, you'd drown when it rained. Isn't life complicated?❜

What happened to the Hell's Angel? Well, the change of image was forced upon me – I couldn't bring the big bike onto Rottnest Island, so I had to use a bicycle to get round like everyone else.

SWIMMING WITH DOLPHINS

Roughly 50 kilometres south of Perth is the beach resort of Rockingham. The area is famous for dolphins and I set out to sea in search of the beautiful creatures. I've always been a little wary of the sea – I've always felt we humans don't have any place there. It took millions of years of evolution to get us out of the place and the first thing we do is run back in. However, being a bit of a hippy, the idea of swimming with dolphins and all that karma enhancement overrode my initial hesitation.

There's something about the idea of swimming with dolphins that is very appealing. No doubt there are all sorts of deep psychological reasons but I'm game, even though I've been told that there are some very large stingrays in the area. I practised a bit of deep breathing before I took the plunge. Apparently it's vital to remain confident in the water as they can sense fear.

It was astonishing, and without a shadow of a doubt one of the most exhilarating experiences of my life. There were dolphins within inches of my face. I'm sure that they could tell I was a hippy. There was an incredible relationship between the dolphins and my instructor. He has worked with them for six years and told me that when a female recently gave birth she bought the calf to show him. There are stranger things in heaven and earth!

❝I don't think people belong in the sea. I mean, we don't get sharks coming and biting us in the street. When you hear a shark ate a person, where do you think that person was? *In the sea!*❞

Yes, it's me, as I approach a friendly dolphin. It was a really fantastic experience swimming with them – I'm sure they recognized an old hippy. 'Yeah, man – how's it with you?'

JIMMY PIKE

In recent years Australia has witnessed a real explosion of interest in Aboriginal art. Australians seem to have finally fallen in love with their country, all its natural splendour and the heritage of its indigenous people. During the tour, I had the privilege of meeting Jimmy Pike, one of Australia's most celebrated and respected artists.

Jimmy is an elder of the Walmajarri people, an ancient, nomadic people who live in Western Australia's Great Sandy Desert. Born in the 1940s, Jimmy spent the first years of his life following a traditional nomadic lifestyle travelling from waterhole to waterhole in search of food and water, learning tribal lore and respecting the lessons of the land and its inhabitants. Jimmy's generation was amongst the last to follow that kind of traditional Aboriginal lifestyle. During the 1950s and 1960s the last of the Walmajarri people moved out of the Great Sandy Desert leaving it largely unpopulated. At the age of thirteen Jimmy and his family moved too, into a settlement town where he took a job at a cattle station working for his rations.

Jimmy Pike was later implicated in a murder and sent to Fremantle prison where he was taught art as part of his rehabilitation. There he met British-born psychologist Pat Lowe, whom he was later to marry. It was Pat who introduced him to painting.

The stories, songs and experiences of his youth formed the basis for much of Jimmy's art. His stark and colourful images, records of his culture and heritage, had an immediate impact on all those who saw them. Jimmy and two partners, Stephen Culley and David Wroth, set up Desert Designs to introduce his work to a wider audience.

During the early 1980s Jimmy entered the commercial art market, initially with black and white linocuts. His subjects are the desert land-scape, and the animal and plant life there, and symbolic features such as the waterholes, which form such an integral part of the Aboriginal experience of life and death.

In 1986 Jimmy returned, with his wife Pat, to the Great Sandy Desert. This return to the desert is being experienced by many Aboriginal people who have gone back to lead a lifestyle which blends the best elements of both worlds. Jimmy lives on the outskirts of the desert and makes frequent journeys deeper into the Outback to seek inspiration.

Left and overleaf: My meeting with Jimmy Pike, one of Australia's most talented and respected Aboriginal artists.

THE PINNACLES

The Nambung National Park, 250 kilometres north of Perth, is a flat featureless desert speckled all over with bizarre phallic structures called the Pinnacles. There are all sorts of wild and wacky theories to explain the phenomenon: perhaps it's a petrified forest, the ruins of a city or the graves of shipwrecked sailors – but in the desert? Much less fancifully, it's believed that they are limestone formations created over millions of years. It's a brilliant place, and the pinnacles themselves range from little stumps just a few centimetres high to ones that are over four metres in height. But like all these strange deserted places it has become a hugely popular tourist spot with some of the tours just taking the 3-kilometre-loop drive through the area without even stopping.

New Age hippies descend on the place in their thousands for the peace and tranquillity, although presumably there's not a lot of it to be had at times like that – which is hilarious when you think about it. All over the world are these monuments of natural wonders which attract the weirdest people. There seems to be some strange and magnetic forces pulling dishevelled old hippies into their spell, and then forcing them to act in a very peculiar manner indeed. It must be the sight of all that erectness. Who knows?

> ❛When the Jehovah's Witnesses come knocking at your front door, shout at them, "Are you a Jehovah's Witness?"
> When they go "yes", then say back, "I'm going to open this door in five seconds, and I'm naked and I've got a big erection – the choice is yours. Five, four, three ..."
> I guarantee they'll be specks in the distance when you open the door.❜

Right and overleaf: The amazing scenery of the Pinnacles in the Nambung National Park. The place seems to attract the weirdest people.

Television is OK if you're telling people the weather and all that, or if it's a scripted show or play or documentary where absolutely everything is prepared beforehand. But people like me don't really belong in television, unless you're being interviewed by somebody good, like Clive James who's also funny and inventive, then something spontaneous might happen as you're talking. Most of the time I don't like comedy on television. I think television kills comedy as it has certain requirements. TV producers will ask, 'Could you give me six and a half minutes?' But comedy isn't like that.

Televised comedy becomes banal because it has to fit between the commercials. It has to fit into weird time requirements because the weatherman has to come on. I've often felt that comedy on television would be much healthier if it were open-ended. Stick it on at one in the morning, or at midnight and leave it open-ended. Put the guy on in concert, and he can finish when he's finished, not when it's time to tell you about beans and soap powder. However, comedy on radio works excellently because it doesn't usually have to meet the same requirements. Radio is a good medium because a lot of the fantasy is left to you. You can only hear the guy's voice and you make your own pictures.

BRISBANE

Queensland is the Sunshine State of Australia and very popular with tourists because of the incredible climate and some truly magnificent natural features: the Great Barrier Reef, Fraser Island, and the wet tropics rainforest to the far north. The state has actively pursued tourism over recent years, trying to establish itself as Australia's Florida. Queenslanders are a very conservative bunch, and Southern Australians joke that when you visit Queensland 'you should turn your watch back an hour and your mind twenty years'. They even have a bizarre law which forbids bartenders from serving sexual perverts.

Brisbane – or 'Brissy' – is a city of contradictions. Modern sky-scrapers tower above low brownstone buildings. Queensland's capital, the 'world's biggest country town', has undergone some rapid redevel-opment and is very 'upwardly mobile'. Pavement cafés teem with fat blokes who don't give a xxxx, while Gold Coast surfers ride high on the crest of a wave. This is a lively and scenic city, but the dominant aspect of life in Brisbane is the heat – Brisbane's sub-tropical climate means that temperatures rarely drop below 20°C.

Brisbane is an extremely hospitable place with a relaxed atmos-phere – most of the time, but I found myself in a lot of trouble here on my first visit to Oz. I was on stage at the Guildhall and a guy – who was a Scottish Australian prison officer, a deadly cocktail – leapt up on stage and smacked me in the mouth, saying 'My wife's ears are not garbage cans.' I fell on my arse, the place was in uproar, the police were called and the whole episode was a complete nightmare. To be honest, I've lied so much about that time over the years and exaggerated it out of all proportion, so that I really don't know what the truth is – which happens to me quite a lot. My real life and my act intermingle so much that I find myself believing the myth and the truth gets conveniently lost.

Despite that episode, I do like it here. It's hot and sweaty and sexy. I've always appreciated humidity, I absolutely love it. The first thing I do on holiday is switch the air-conditioning off so my body regulates itself. Brisbane is very close to the Gold Coast – 32 kilometres of white beaches and rolling surf – but the city itself is based around the mean-dering Brisbane River. The bridge over the river had barely been built before people were throwing themselves off it. My theory is that you should do a recce first – try a bungy jump, see how you like it. If it's not to your taste, there's always the gas oven.

Brissy – hot and humid, the 'world's biggest country town.'

This is a survivor, one of Brisbane's old houses. The march of the high rise is relentless.

The city centre is quite spectacular, with glistening high-rise office blocks alongside more traditional Queensland architecture. It's a jolly-looking place but I preferred it before all the redevelopment. I first came here about twenty years ago and things were all a lot closer to the ground. Call me a sentimental old fool but I preferred it then. Now it's the fastest-growing city in Australia and high-rises are shooting up all over the place. That's progress for you.

Brisbane was first established as the place where they sent all the really hard-core convicts – the ones who continued to break the law even after being transported to Australia. The Brits thought that Sydney was too soft so they sent the real hard guys to Brisbane and treated them dreadfully. It seemed a good idea to send them to the tropical north which was, at that time, occupied by three Aboriginal tribes – who at first were friendly. The colony was named after the Scottish Governor of New South Wales, Sir Thomas Brisbane. The new convict settlement was established on the site of Brisbane's present-day city centre and was later thrown open to free settlers.

Yet the dark days of Brisbane's nightmarish beginnings continued, not least with strong Aboriginal resistance from the late 1820s to the white occupation. This violence even resulted in 1830 in the slaying by Aborigines of the legendary Captain Patrick Logan, brutal commander of the Stadbroke Island concentration camp.

Over the last decade the city has tried very hard to shake off its tag as a dull, provincial backwater. In 1988 Brisbane put on Expo 88, an event which attracted 18 million visitors and put the city on the world map. Today the site of Expo 88 has been renamed the South Bank Parklands. Within the parklands, the Gondwana Sanctuary was created, set around a massive synthetic rock. It is home to rainforest plants, native birds, reptiles and beasties, including crocodiles, koalas, possums and snakes. As you know, I'm a man of simple pleasures who likes nothing more than strolling casually to work. The Parklands are on the way to the gig from the hotel and you can walk through this incredible manmade rainforest right in the centre of Brisbane. It's absolutely great.

The local delicacy is the Queensland mud crab. Also known as the mangrove crab, it's seen on menus throughout Brisbane. Living on mud flats and in tidal waters, especially those lined with mangroves, they can grow as large as 2 kilos. The 'Queensland muddie' tastes delicious and could tempt me away from vegetarianism for good.

There is a lot of funny wildlife in Brisbane. Any place that has a poisonous spider, the red back, which lives in the lavatory pan is a nightmare! Being bitten in the scrotum is just not my idea of a good time. Arghh!!

I tend to slip in and out of vegetarianism. I have a real problem with it – you see I don't like vegetarians. I find them a bit youth-hostelish: "A stranger is just a friend you don't know yet." Vegans are even worse. When I talk to a vegan I get an overwhelming desire to bite a live pig's arse.

121

QUEENSLAND HOUSES

We all know what a used-car lot looks like. In Queensland, they have used-house lots. Houses in Queensland have their own unique design which has been adapted to cope with the hot and humid climate. The 'Queenslander' style of house doesn't have foundations dug but instead it rests on top of wooden stumps. You just drive along the freeway to your nearest dealer. All the houses are stacked on wooden pallets and you can drive up and say, 'OK, I'll take the yellow one!' Give the man your details and he'll deliver your house and stumps to the location of your choice.

Opposite: Some of Brissy's old houses have beautiful wrought-iron work.

Below: Roll up and buy one!

You can even buy a 'Queenslander' fully furnished. You order your furniture, it's installed at the lot, tied down for the journey and delivered to where your front door will be. All you have to do is roll up and live in the thing.

The houses come in all shapes and sizes, but they're all basically a wooden box, raised up on pole supports with a high corrugated-iron roof, and broad verandahs or balconies. The further north you go, the higher off the ground they get. The stumps which support the houses off the ground are there to help get air circulating around the house, to improve ventilation and cut through the stifling humidity.

The biggest danger to the stability of these houses is posed by the millions of termites which like nothing better than a good old chomp on the supporting stumps. The locals have a very simple and effective method of dealing with this threat – they simply place a metal plate between the stumps and the base of the house. People here obviously take stump rot very seriously indeed. To test for stump rot you have to hit the stump hard with a hammer. If it sinks in, the ants have been at it. If it bounces back and smacks you in the face then it's perfectly all right.

FRASER ISLAND

This is the biggest sand island in the world, over 120 kilometres long, with its own rainforest. Driving on the sandy tracks is a bit like driving in snow.

Pile Valley has some huge trees which, because they are sheltered right here, grow straight upwards to a tremendous height. Some of them reach seventy metres. They are known as turpentine trees but their real name is the satinay tree; their timber was used to line the Suez Canal in the 1920s and the London Docks after the Second World War. The sap has the same qualities as turpentine which stops marine life affecting the wood. There was once such a demand for them that people began to worry about their survival. In the 1970s and 1980s there were a lot of demonstrations about felling them, and now they are protected.

Lake McKenzie has a good Scottish name, but it's also sometimes called 'the blue lake', for obvious reasons. It's a freshwater lake and the fine white sand under the freshwater gives it a lovely turquoisey colour. I decided to go for a swim. I was told there were turtles in it but I didn't care – it was delicious and delightful.

6 Children don't like scenery. They just don't get it. I took my children to Scotland in a camper van for a holiday. We were surrounded by the most incredible scenery – mountains, rivers, stags, salmon jumping. You name it – we had it. "There you are girls," I said. "What do you think?" They looked all around them and then back at me, with blank looks. "What? Where?" They didn't have a clue what I was talking about. You have to be taught that scenery is *nice*. Mountains and trees, in that order, are *nice*. 9

Some of the huge trees in Pile Valley on Fraser Island.

Left: On beautiful Fraser
Island, music and solitude
at sundown.

Above: An aerial vew of the blue
lake, Lake McKenzie.

Right: I strip off for a swim.

It can be hard being away from my family so often, but it does have its good points. I miss them a lot but you can't spend the whole day missing the family. You have to just get on with it. I'm sure it's the same for people in the armed forces. You go off, do what you're supposed to do for a living, and then go back to the family for extended periods of twenty-four hours a day. When I'm home, I'm the cook of the house. I make all the lunches and ferry the kids to school, and chauffeur them between friends' houses and home.
I think that love is the secret. If you are loved by people whom you love, you don't miss them in the way that you would if there was any uncertainty about the situation. I'm very lucky, I'm loved and I love my troops back home, so it's easy.

I've never become an adult. On one side it frightens
me that I'm kind of incomplete. I'm a child-man.
Physically I'm an adult, I'm as adult as you get. I'm getting old,
I'm going grey and wrinkly. But mentally I've remained a child.
I'm immature. I've been looked after all my life. First by my sister
when I was a child, and then, as I got older, various organizations
looked after me like the Cubs and the Scouts. And then I was in the
shipyards where all your decisions were made for you. And now I
do this and I have a crew of people and a manager and management
who look after me. For instance, I don't know how to buy a house.
I've never bought a car. The office has always bought it for me.
I phone the office and say, 'Look, I think I need another car.
I'd like to trade this in and get another one,' and someone goes
and does it. I don't know how to do it. I've never phoned
someone about an ad in *Exchange and Mart* and talked about
an Allegro. My wife knows how to do all that. She pays my
mortgage. She phones the gardener. She knows who to phone,
and who to see and who to talk to, and she keeps me well
out of the way of it in case I bugger it up.

My children have Australian passports because my wife is
an Australian and when she had the children, we weren't married.
People always used to ask Pamela when we were going to get
married. She always said the same thing, 'When the children are
old enough to enjoy the wedding.' The three girls were
bridesmaids at the wedding and they had a fantastic time.

COOBER PEDY

Coober Pedy is just so Australian. As soon as I arrived here I had an overwhelming desire to sing 'Waltzing Matilda' and dig out my old Rolf Harris albums.

Almost midway between the coast and Alice Springs, 860 kilometres north of Adelaide, Coober Pedy is a dismally inhospitable place, where the summer temperature is often 50°C. The heat is indescribable – I can honestly say I have never been this hot in my entire life. Coober Pedy is the closest Australia has to offer to a true 'frontier town'. The mines leave a bit of a mess but who's going to see it? The population of 2500 is made up of fifty-two different nationalities and includes about 400 Aborigines. Coober Pedy – the name comes from an Aboriginal phrase meaning 'white feller's burrow' – is the opal capital of the world. This is mining country.

I think opals look a bit plastic but some people love them and just can't get enough. One of the miners told me that the Japanese, in particular, are 'opal crazy', with the rare black and crystal opals commanding incredible sums of money.

Opals were first discovered here, or rather stumbled upon, by a gold prospector called William Hutchison in 1915. The township expanded a great deal following the First World War, when soldiers returning from the front found a much more lucrative use for their trench-digging skills.

In the early days the miners dug manually, beginning at the top of a man-made shaft and simply digging down until they reached the bottom. Despite the many thousands of mines, there are no corporate mining interests here. Deals are done pretty much in the same way as they were done eighty years ago, with a couple of guys sealing a deal with a handshake and a few drinks in the local pub.

Opal mining in Coober Pedy has continued in this 'cottage industry' low-tech way. Today the most sophisticated machine they use is called a 'bogger'. A tunnelling device swirls down the mine and tips out all the waste behind it and then the bogger comes along and scoops it all out to form a perfect tunnel.

When this tunnelling system is used, the miners then follow white seams which run on the side of the tunnel walls, hoping that the seam will lead them to the opals. More often than not all they find is gypsum, which has no commercial value. It's always intrigued me why some

Coober Pedy is the place for opal mining. The mines don't do a lot for the landscape, but the heat makes this place so unbearable, who's going to be around to see the mess?

stones are placed at high value and others are just ignored. I know that the value can depend on how rare the stone is, but I still reckon that if Princess Diana could be encouraged to wear gypsum jewellery, she would start a trend that would send the price of gypsum rocketing through the roof. It would certainly be good news for Coober Pedy.

> ‘Why does Rolf Harris want his kangaroo tied down? Has anybody ever explained that? It sounds filthy to me.
> *'Tie me kangaroo down sport, tie me kangaroo down ...'*
> I've never figured it out.
> *'Shake me wallaby's juice, loose ...'*

The Aborigines have no tradition of mining because they fear being underground. Jolly right too! Another of their traditional beliefs is that their manifestation of the Devil lives under the ground. In Aboriginal mythology he's depicted as half-man and half-serpent, a hideous beast which lures people to their deaths by laying a trail of shiny, desirable stones which they follow, never to be seen again!

Some of the old mining shafts are a bit creepy. In common with mining communities the world over, the residents of Coober Pedy today hold superstitious beliefs that the creaking and groaning that comes from the old workings is the ghosts of dead miners.

Anyone can have a go at searching for opals. All you need is a prospecting permit from the Mines Department in Adelaide. Or you can 'fossick' through the mining outcasts for any overlooked stones. In Coober Pedy, this is known as 'noodling'. Some people actually make a living there just noodling though the scree – or 'mullock', a Scottish-sounding word – just finding interesting bits and pieces. I think I was born to noodle.

Don't make the mistake of thinking that opals are plentiful and just sitting around waiting to be dug up. The last really big strikes were in the 1970s. These days the opal deposits are so scattered and scarce that the residents of Coober Pedy seem to spend more time working out dodges and scams to beat the system than actually digging for opals. For example, although mining in the town centre itself was banned years ago, you will frequently find people building extensions to their houses which strangely seem to require deeper than normal excavation! It can be extremely frustrating, with many miners going weeks and months without even a sniff of an opal. When word gets out of a find, everyone descends on the same area.

I decided to give this mining thing a go. Basically, you need to mix some diesel with some other secret ingredients and put it in a wine

bottle with a fuse. Light the fuse, run away and wait for the bang. It will perhaps come as no surprise to learn that explosives are the largest cause of injury in the mines. A week before my visit a man had blown his hand off and another had been buried alive because of mishandled explosives.

Explosives are also used above ground. In Coober Pedy, some people use them to settle their disputes. If you upset someone, it's not uncommon to return home and find your house has been blown up. In this heat tempers tend to run very high, and since 1987 the police station has been blown up at least twice. I was told that bombs have also been set off in the court house, the Acropolis restaurant and the offices of the local newspaper. It's all right folks, I didn't find any opals, honestly.

Mining has left its mark on Coober Pedy. The desolate Outback landscape is littered with the junk and detritus of mining activity – twisted metal, abandoned drills and all sorts of other old equipment. It should come as no surprise to learn that Coober Pedy's apocalyptic backdrop was used as the location for filming some of the most effective scenes in *Mad Max: Beyond Thunderdome*, the sci-fi thriller with Mel Gibson.

We filmed the opal mining and I learned about 'noodling' and explosives.

An underground home in Coober Pedy, complete with private drinks bar.

Opposite: The best headstone on a grave I've ever seen: a beer keg printed with the legend 'Have a drink on me.'

To escape the blinding sun and heat, many of the residents of Coober Pedy live in 'dug outs'. The majority of these are simply exhausted mines, however a few cave dwellings have been 'purpose cut' out of the rock.

I had a look at one of these. It began life in the 1930s as an underground garage to house the local mail van. Then in 1964 a woman called Faye and two of her friends, all ex-army and aged in their sixties, dug away at the garage and enlarged it until they had created a home.

It was completely incredible and fantastically cool. You think of cave dwellers and you imagine people leading a really basic existence, living on beetles and grubs. But this house completely turns that idea on its head. The master bedroom has an en suite bathroom. The whole house is well-ventilated and lit and there's even a wine cellar – and all this is carved out of the solid rock. The most everyday, mundane things appear so odd – a cooker or a coffee pot suddenly seem really bizarre.

The *pièce de résistance* had to be an indoor swimming-pool. Despite the furnace-like temperature outside, they actually have to heat the water in the pool with a system of solar panels, because the rock cools the water so incredibly successfully.

I could have lived there, but I was pipped to the post. It had been empty for some time and, the week before my visit, a couple who were passing through visited the house, fell in love with it and are all set to move in.

As I said, Coober Pedy is in the middle of nowhere, and you have to make a mental adjustment to life in a parallel universe. If life here is slightly off-beat, then so is death. Since 1965 it has been the responsibility of the police to bury the dead.

The graveyard here has a headstone that I love. It commemorates Karl Bratz who died in 1992. His grave is marked by his hat and a beer keg printed with the legend 'Have a drink on me'. Karl must have had a terminal illness and time to plan for the big day – even to the point of getting his coffin in advance. It was made of corrugated iron and it resided, until he needed it, in the front room, where he used it as a wine rack.

Many of the graves are very simple. People here lead a pretty basic existence, and when they die the tradition is for the town to have a whip-round to give the bereaved a little holiday or a gift. I like their simplicity – often there's just a white cross – they have a lot of dignity. I have never before seen a grave decorated with a T-shirt, but the grave of Ivy Lange is adorned with a white one which shows a black hand and the words, 'Reconciliation, coming together, the answers are within us all.'

‘I've made my wife promise to put "Jesus Christ, is that the time already?" on my gravestone. I'm not going to be there anyway – I'll be scattered all over Loch Lomond. She had a bit of a problem with it, so I've told her that the only other thing I'll settle for is *tiny* writing in the middle of a huge stone. The writing will be so small that people will have to get up really close to read: "You're standing on my balls."’

DESERT GOLF

I have never understood the point of golf, or for that matter, golfers. I can only suppose that it was intended as a joke which would go some way towards explaining the V-neck sweaters with lions on them and the tartan polyester trousers.

In Coober Pedy, there is a spectacularly surreal example of a golf course. Slap bang in the middle of the Outback is the Desert Golf Course, but you'd be hard pushed to find grassy 'fairways', 'water hazards' and verdant 'greens'. The greens are black and speckled with discarded tyres, the *least* green fairways I've ever seen, and the tees are a sort of portable box arrangement covered with a strip of Astro-turf. You needn't ever worry about getting caught in the sand as you're permanently in it!

I'm standing on the green of the ninth hole of Coober Pedy golf course – but there isn't a speck of green to be seen in the whole place except for a few lonely looking trees.

After teeing off, the golfers pick up their strip of Astro-turf and carry it with them around the course. This really is crazy golf.

When the Scots invented golf all those years ago, they played with balls made of leather and stuffed with feathers – I'm sure that no one was meant to take it seriously. Desert golf is what that kind of mental illness leads to. I say, give the golf courses to the homeless.

'Call them what you will: wallies, geeks, cedrics, gunzels. They are all people who've completely narrowed down their interests so that they know a lot about something that nobody else gives a shit about. They've all got on the Internet now – that great anorak in the sky. You know why they're on the Internet, don't you? Because you wouldn't speak to them in the pub, that's why.'

THE DOG FENCE

In this book I have shown you many things. Some high, some low, some beautiful, some colourful, some animal, some mineral – now, ladies and gentlemen, may I proudly present the longest fence in the world, about 5600 kilometres long. This is the Australian equivalent of Hadrian's Wall and it serves a very essential purpose. It's the famous dog fence. On one side is the northern cattle territory where the dingoes live, and on the other side, the south-eastern side, live the sheep. The fence has been erected to prevent the dingoes doing what they do best, eating sheep. On a good night out a pair of dingoes can kill dozens of sheep, so a pack could devastate a flock. Hence the fence.

The rolling land and huge sky here reminds me of Texas. There's something about a great deal of nothing which is very impressive. It makes you feel small and insignificant, which is never a bad thing as it's very good to know your place. Politicians should be brought out here at regular intervals just to be made to feel insignificant.

'I was devastated when Frank Zappa died because he was planning to go into politics. Can you imagine that? Frank Zappa the President of the United States of America! In my dreams. He was my hero. He lived in the same street as me in Los Angeles. I always wanted to knock on his door but I was too scared. After he died I was walking the dog and I went past his house. His wife came outside and said, "Are you Billy Connolly? Frank was your biggest fan." I thought "Oh Jesus, I could have been vice-president."'

COOKING DAMPER

When in the Outback you have to know how to look after yourself, so I tried my hand at a spot of bush cooking. It was an invigorating mix of bread, tea and kangaroo scrotum.

Damper bread is an essential of life in the Outback and is made from flour, water, salt and margarine, to a recipe that goes back centuries. It is commonly cooked in a pan over an open fire but I improvised with some tin foil, which will no doubt disgust damper-bread-makers the world over. Whilst my bread was cooking, or rather burning as I was to discover later, I put a billycan on the fire to make my tea. I also consulted an ancient manuscript which shares with its readers the magical delight of creating something with your own hands for a loved one – the 'family jewels purse'.

I just know you'll want to make it. Here's the recipe:

One large red kangaroo (deceased)
One bootlace
A stick (about 2.5 centimetres thick)
A billycan of tea leaves and sludge
A stone, or 'yonnie' to give it its Australian name,
*   about 7.5 centimetres across*

Cooking damper over my campfire in the Outback.

First, take the kangaroo and cut off its scrotum – be sure to include a good 10 centimetres diameter of the belly skin too. Turn the scrotum inside out, and put the 'yonnie' in the hairy bottom bit. Put the stick in until it touches the stone, then tie it all up with string, rub in a good handful of salt, and hang it in a well-ventilated place to dry.

When dry – sorry, there seems to be no prescribed time for this – you'll have to use your own judgement – remove all the fat from the skin, take out the stone and start the tanning process. Let me assure you this sort of tanning has nothing to do with poking your scrotum outside to 'catch some rays' – in fact it's far more tasteful than that. It involves putting the scrotum in your billycan with all your old tea leaves and sludge for about three weeks – not forgetting to stir it every day.

After this, dry it again – rubbing it often to make the skin soft and supple. The easy bit follows – make incisions all around the top to make holes through which you thread your boot lace to form the draw-string. I am told that when you now turn it inside out you will have a really useful, soft, hairy purse.

What a fabulous gift for a loved one! I'm also told that it makes a wonderful tobacco pouch – well, it would certainly be a good conversation piece. There you have it, a 'family jewels purse' made with items readily available in the Outback!

Meanwhile, back at the ranch I set to on the cooked damper. It looked ruined – burned to a cinder on the outside. But when I broke it open, the smell and the taste were delicious. My tea was equally successful. A handy hint is to swing the billycan around your head to make the tea leaves settle at the bottom.

❝Whether you're male or female, I guarantee that you'll be outraged by the following. It's the most chauvinist thing I've ever heard but it's just so Scottish, it's brilliant. I was was told this story by a make-up artist. She was making her Grandad a nice cup of tea and she asked him how many sugars he took. He said, "I don't know, ask your Granny."❞

Hello Mate! I always thought you were only a Billy Tea advertisement!

❝Of an afternoon, I like to partake of a wee fairy cake and a cup of tea. I'm also partial to the odd cappuccino, being an unstoppable trendy. But I always have to think of Al Pacino because I keep forgetting the name of the damn stuff. On more than one occasion, I've asked a waitress for a Robert De Niro.❞

My kids love the fact that I'm famous. They absolutely love it because I can get tickets for anything – that's the main thing as far as they're concerned. I had a part in the Disney film *Pocahontas* and we all went to the première and met Mickey Mouse. The other reason the kids love it is because you get to know other famous people. They couldn't give a toss about me being famous but they love the fact that I have famous friends. I remember taking my daughter to a restaurant and the singer George Michael joined us. My daughter was trembling. She was about twelve at the time and when he left he shook hands with everybody and kissed her goodbye. She just melted.

My daughter went to a tattooist's parlour with her pal who wanted to have her belly-button pierced. She came back and said, 'You must see this guy – he's covered in tattoos.' So I went to look at him. That's another plus-point to being famous. I can just swan in and say, 'Give us a look at your body,' and people will. I was examining all the tattoos and I saw he had parts of his body pierced, and I heard myself say, 'I've always fancied having my nipples pierced.' And he said, 'Well, I'm the very man to do it.'

I went back about a year later – on Father's Day – and I asked him to do it. He asked why I wanted it doing, at my age. So I told him, 'I've always been kind of rebellious and now I'm not. It's boring. I wander about like a civil servant.' And he said, 'Right, let's go.' It was *agony*. I had intended to get them both done but after the first I thought, 'I think one will do for today!' But I kept getting an overwhelming desire to match it up. It's like only wearing one shoe – it's kind of stupid. So I went back a year later to get the other one done.

After he had cleaned it up, he stood back and said something fantastic, 'There you go – one more of us, one less of them.' I thought, 'That's why I did it – because I wanted to be an "us", I'm not comfortable being a "them". I have pierced nipples.'

When I hang up my boots I'll get the old willy pierced. Why not?

ALICE SPRINGS

The Outback is a huge stretch of arid desert that covers more than a third of this continent. To give you an idea, a sort of mental yardstick, we're talking about an area roughly the size of Western Europe or two-thirds the area of the United States. Pretty damned big.

There are four major desert ranges that comprise the Outback: the Great Sandy Desert, the Simpson Desert, the Gibson Desert, and the Great Victoria Desert. It is impossible to comprehend the sheer scale of it all: it's enormous beyond belief. No amount of figures or statistics could prepare you for the experience of standing in the middle of it all.

I had a similarly awe-inspiring experience in Canada – I was 'marooned' in the Arctic for a television programme – me, my banjo and a tent. It was a very odd experience – not unpleasant, just strange. I felt like the only person on Earth. Funnily enough, I wasn't ever frightened – there was something reassuring about being so tiny in the middle of that vast emptiness.

The Outback is the empty core of Australia. The people who live here cling to the edges of the country, near the coast. As a result, the majority of this huge land is empty. An empty, arid, barren world of sand, red dust and strange plants and animals. This is Mad Max country – a world beyond man's control. The Aborigines have an intuitive understanding and respect for the land which they have occupied for thousands of years. But the mysteries of the Outback remain elusive to its white settlers and, particularly, to tourists like myself.

Aside from the huge stretches of land, you can't help being aware of the sky. You get a lot of sky for your money in these parts and it all adds to the feeling of the wide open space. I've travelled to places all over the world and have been dumbfounded by the staggering beauty of a variety of scenery. It all pales into insignificance beside the Outback.

The immense and hostile land area has given rise to a fabulous sense of community and forbearance. There are settlements here but they have had to cope in the face of great adversity.

These are the MacDonnell mountain ranges near Alice Springs. Alice at 'the centre of Australia', is the major town of the Outback and it attracts huge numbers of tourists.

Ever since I read the Nevil Shute novel *A Town Like Alice* I have been intrigued by Alice Springs. I've been to most of the major towns and cities in Australia many times over during my career – but this is my first visit to 'The Alice'. Despite the name, there are no springs at Alice Springs but there is a 'billabong' – a waterhole in the dried-up bed of the Todd River. The population today stands at about 25 000 people, making Alice Springs the largest settlement in the Australian interior.

The town was originally a staging post for the Overland Telegraph Line. The OTL ran across the centre of Australia and provided the first direct line connection to Europe. Originally called Stuart, the settlement was first properly established in 1888 with the advent of the railway. Stuart was designated as the proposed rail head for a new railway link to Adelaide. Because of construction difficulties – sand, sand and more sand – progress was very slow and the town was slow to expand. The railway connection was eventually completed in 1929. By 1933, the town had changed its name to Alice Springs and the population had grown to two hundred.

The railway line to Adelaide proved horrendously unreliable. The track frequently disappeared beneath the sand or was washed away by flash floods. It was not uncommon for trains to arrive three months late. It wasn't really until the 1980s when the railway line was rebuilt and the Stuart Highway was constructed, that the tourists were able to arrive and Alice Springs really discovered prosperity.

Much of its tourist success is down to the marketing people who cottoned on to Alice Spring's location at the geographical centre of Australia and tagged it 'The Centre of the Interior'. The less wholesome publicity of the Ayers Rock Dingo Baby Saga has now faded and Alice makes a very good living from pretending to be near Ayers Rock – in fact the two places are as close together as London and Glasgow.

Alice Spring's social 'season' centres around the cooler months of May to August with highlights such as the Alice Springs Agricultural Show, the Alice Springs Rodeo and the Camel Cup – a series of camel races. The biggest draw and also the most bizarre event has to be the Henley-on-Todd regatta. The course of the race follows the Todd River which is normally bone dry. The race is a team event – the boats

Right: Yes this is the Todd River and this is how it usually looks – bone dry.
Inset: The Henley-on-Todd race in progress along the dry river bed.

are all bottomless so that the crew's legs stick out and they run along the dry river bed. I suspect it's the heat that is responsible for such acts of insanity. The regatta has been cancelled twice because there was water in the river!

I was astonished to learn that Alice Springs has its own winery, located fairly close to the airport. Chateau Hornsby doesn't exactly conjure up images of sophisticated high-living, and the wine has been described as 'more memorable for its novelty than quality'. A polite way, I think, of saying that it's crap.

As the 'Capital of the Interior' Alice Springs is the base for two organizations which have developed to provide services adapted to cope with the scale of the Outback. The famous Royal Flying Doctor Service, which was founded seventy years ago, is responsible for medical care throughout the Outback. Education services are provided by the School of the Air – not a flying school, but a school on the airwaves. Set up in 1951 it uses the radio network established by the flying doctors to provide an education for children scattered all over the area. In addition to the radio school, correspondence courses play an important part in education here.

Alice Springs is an extraordinary place, and it's much more modern and civilized than I had expected. It isn't the frontier town I had pictured, full of drunk people doing crazy things. Coming here certainly brings home the reality of living in the Outback – a world where you can live over 500 kilometres from the nearest doctor or supermarket, you rely on a fortnightly postal delivery, and school is sitting in front of a radio!

> ❛I saw a French woman on TV who's 120 years old which makes her the oldest person alive. She seemed like a smashing person. She said, "I think God forgot me". And then, this was my favourite line, she said, "I only have one wrinkle and I'm sitting on it." God, I hope I'm making jokes when I'm 120.❜

Alice Springs – 'Capital of the Interior'.

My first ambition was to be a tramp. I was desperate to be a hairy tramp, wandering around the place being given sandwiches by people. My reading book when I was a little boy had a story about a tramp. He was a nice-looking man with a beard and a big coat. The tramp knocked on a kind woman's door and she gave him a jam sandwich. I thought that would be a great life. I was sick with envy because my people used to give me marmalade sandwiches and I couldn't bear marmalade. The tramp got the red stuff, the raspberry gear. It was obvious what I had to do so I thought, 'It's a tramp's life for me.' My father was really befuddled by it. Later, I told him I wanted to be a steward at sea. A lot of Glaswegians joined the Merchant Navy and went to sea. I said, 'I'd like to be a steward,' and my father replied, 'They're all homosexuals, I wouldn't advise you to do that.' So I came back some time later and announced I wanted to be an actor. He said, 'You can't, they're all homosexuals.' I couldn't be an actor so I became a welder instead. I used to tell the other welders that I became a welder to avoid becoming a homosexual.

When I meet Prince Charles, which is really quite rare, I tend not to talk about his marital problems. I talk about other subjects. I try and look intelligent, you know, which is really difficult for me. I wet my hair and all that. Of course, he finds all the media attention, like everybody in that position, a terrible strain. I did anyway when it happened to me. You get all the same slimeballs climbing up the pipes outside your house, you know? I remember lying in bed and seeing a guy take my picture from the roof across the road. I thought, 'What was I doing? How long has he been there? … Oh my God!' And after that I would start pulling the sheets down and showing my bare arse. Have you ever done that? Do it if the cleaning lady's coming into your room in the hotel, pretend to be asleep and do that …

'Will Billy Connolly punch another photographer?' Well, you can't punch them all, but you can punch some of them and it's delightful. I would advise anybody, 'Have a go, whack one, just to see how you feel,' because they never gang up on you. His mates all take pictures of you punching him. There's a great game you can play if you ever find yourself hounded by the paparazzi. When photographers take your photo they walk backwards. If you do it properly you can aim them at lampposts and dustbins.

DARWIN

The Northern Territory is known in Aussie parlance as 'The Territory' or 'NT.' It covers a sixth of the continent but only one percent of Australians actually live there.

From the burnt south to the tropical north ('The Top End'), these extreme climates, together with its distance and isolation from the rest of developed Australia, all add to the tough, maverick, 'lawless frontier' mythology which The Territory still encourages today. It has some of the oldest inhabited Aborigine sites and a quarter of the population is Aboriginal. Nearly half of The Territory is owned by Aborigines.

Dame Edna Everage once remarked, 'Darwin is a virus, not a city; there is no cure.' It is one of the northernmost points of the continent and is the only significant settlement in the 'The Top End'. It's a city of contrasts and a great place to perform, with a wonderfully humid, sweaty climate. The average annual temperature is in the 30s and the city operates at a leisurely and laid-back pace. I visited in November, the hottest month of the year, and a time of frequent thunderstorms. Darwin has over ninety 'thunderdays' every year between September and March – making it one of the world's most lightning-prone areas.

There are two seasons in Darwin – wet and dry. The dry season between May and October turns the land brown and is responsible for a good many bush fires. The wet season is a time for thunderstorms and monsoons which drown the region in up to two metres of water. During the wet season Darwin and the surrounding area are green and dust-free, the barrumundi fishing is at its best, and there are some fantastic storms which render many of the dirt roads impassable.

Darwin is a neat, modern place, largely thanks to Cyclone Tracy which struck on Christmas Eve in 1974. The city had been bombed by the Japanese during the Second World War, and Tracy once more razed it to the ground. Three-quarters of the population were evacuated, and those not too traumatized by the experience returned to brand new homes and developments costing around $A700 million. This is still a popular destination for cyclones – one every few years.

Darwin is on the edge of the continent. Whenever you come to the end of any country there are people wandering around looking lost. Darwin is just like that. It's difficult to pinpoint a single cause but I suspect that the Darwin fascination with the amber nectar would account for it. Excessive drinking is a way of life and they drink more beer per head than anywhere in the world. The Darwin 'stubbie' is the largest bottle of beer in the world too, holding nearly four pints (2.25 litres)!

Darwin – hot, humid and the thirstiest city in the world.

CROCODILES

On the banks of the Adelaide River, in the Kakadu National Park just outside Darwin, I went in search of crocodiles, which wasn't too hard as they are in plentiful supply in these parts. We had a boat, a load of pig heads to use as bait, a crocodile expert in charge, and I wore a special crocodile-skin headband which I thought would endear me to my quarry.

Crocodiles are a very real fact of life here. Darwin has a crocodile farm to research and monitor the crocodile population. It's also the main supplier of crocodile meat – a local delicacy.

There are two types of crocodile – freshies and salties. Freshies live in fresh water and are distinguishable by their narrow noses and neat spiky teeth. They can grow up to three metres in length and live on seafood, birds and small mammals. Salties can live in both fresh and salt water and they can grow to an impressive seven metres long. They're nasty broad-nosed beasts which frequently attack humans, buffaloes and even each other. Nobody picks a fight with them.

Salties are clever and vicious predators. They can remain inert and impassive, looking like dead wood for days at a time, but when they do strike, they can be very fast. You can't assume it's safe to swim just because there are no warning signs around. The signs have become very popular with a certain kind of idiot tourist who frequently uproots them and takes them home as souvenirs.

The crocodile safari is a fascinating experience. The bait – a pig's eye fillet – proved irresistible. Despite all those teeth, crocodiles can't chew, so they store their catches until they rot and then rip off strips. Generally they are said to prefer fish and mud crabs to rotting meat but I wasn't taking any chances.

❝I used to be a blue grass banjo player. I could lead you in a sing-song:
Oh, old McDonald was dyslexic, E O I O E ...❞

Before this trip, I had only ever seen dead crocodiles and I found them slightly revolting. But seeing them in their natural habitat you can't fail to be impressed. You must also respect their incredible hunting skills – they are perfectly-evolved killers with nearly 160 million years practice. I might be able to play the banjo properly if I had that much practice.

Here I am actually taking part in hanging bait outside the boat to attract crocodiles. Yes, I do think the heat in Darwin affects the brain.

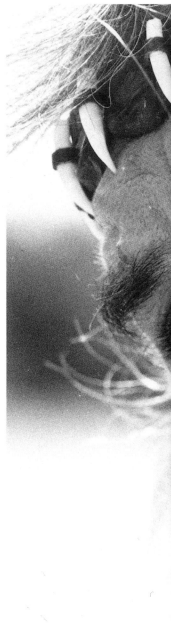

What do you think of my crocodile headband? What do you mean I look a bit worried?
Wouldn't you, if the guy above had jumped up within inches of *your* nose?

BARRAMUNDI FISHING

I'm here in Shady Camp, outside Darwin, and I've come to catch a barramundi. They taste superb. It's probably my favourite fish to eat apart from haddock, but I'm not going to eat this one, I just want to catch one. It's the most beautiful fish, so I'm going out with some experts to see what happens. The barramundi is Australia's most highly prized native sport fish. They have a reputation for fighting like crazy – the battle can easily last ten minutes – and ends, more often than not, with the barramundi escaping.

The barramundi has a pretty wild sex life. Females spawn around the river mouths so that the eggs get washed by the tide into the coastal swamps. The fish then head for freshwater and male fish change sex to enable the whole spawning cycle to start again.

To the amateur eye, I might look like just another guy with dodgy hair out fishing. But any expert could tell you that this is Man the Hunter at work. Just a couple of seconds ago, a red dragon fly landed right in front of me. I didn't move a muscle. I didn't cry. I didn't run for cover and I didn't wet my trousers. Pretty soon I'll have a huge beastie on the end of this line and I won't flinch because I'm made of stern stuff. The stuff that made this country great! This morning I was watching TV, a nature programme. They showed a Jesus bird, a little black bird with a red head that walks on lily pads. It's called a Jesus bird because it looks as if it's walking on the water and I've just spotted one. I was so pleased with myself. You know when you see something on film, you think it's for other people and you'll never see anything like that.

This is just so brilliant. I love the feel of it all. I love the fact that we're under a lovely blue sky with white fluffy clouds and over on the horizon – yonder – there's a huge storm brewing. It's the most dramatic and beautiful thing. Again, it lets you know just how insignificant you actually are. It's a very, very good thing.

> ❝The human race has been set up. Someone, somewhere, is playing a practical joke on us. Apparently, women need to feel loved to have sex. Men need to have sex to feel loved. How do we ever get started?❞

There was a thunderclap then. I've always loved thunder. My father used to tell me it was God moving his furniture around the room. When my children were small I would take them outside to a little porch with big cushions and we would sit and applaud the storm and give it marks out of ten.

I've just watched two dragonflies mating. It's at times like this, when there's nothing happening, that a man's mind turns to sex. You know what they say, the devil finds work for idle hands.

God's way of dealing with it is to send a cold shower. It's incredible how quickly the weather can change here. The storm I talked about earlier has now caught up with us. I must say it's done the trick, I'm now concentrating totally on catching a fish.

I did catch one – a little beauty. What we would call 'frying-pan size' in Scotland.

Above and overleaf: There's nothing I like better than a good storm and you get the best ones in the world in this country.

❛I'm obsessed with staying power, trying to make sex last for a decent length of time. Men have to be very careful not to let themselves go. All the while they're having sex, they have to try and think about something other than sex so that they last longer. Isn't it strange to think of the woman screaming, "Oh yes, oh yes, more, more, harder, faster, ooooooooh YES!" and all the while the guy's reciting his nine-times tables. Well, that's what works for me anyway. I once got to "eight nines are seventy-two" and had to do a lap of honour, bare-arsed around the bed.❜

THE ABORIGINES

There are nearly 250 000 Aboriginal people living in Australia. They are still the single most disadvantaged group in the country, and it's only been in the last twenty years or so that these people were granted basic rights. In the early days of the colony the indigenous population was unilaterally dispossessed of its land. Aborigines were persecuted, marginalized and placed in penal colonies. The diseases that the white man brought with him from Europe decimated the people and, even as recently as the 1950s, outbreaks of flu and measles severely affected desert people. Those who survived the diseases lost their land and their freedom.

The long history of persecution led to a perception in the early 1900s that the Aborigines were a dying race, yet by the 1930s it was apparent that the numbers were actually increasing. Many of these people were still confined to government-allotted reserves or worked as poorly-paid cattlemen or domestic servants. In the 1950s a policy began where children were removed from their Aborigine mothers and put into the care of white foster parents as part of a misguided assimilation strategy. It didn't work and these children are clearly now disaffected adults who, quite rightly, feel robbed of contact with their natural families and culture.

There is still a major government inquiry underway into this mad period of 'taking the children away', as it is known, but ironically this policy was one of the key issues which forced the Aboriginal groups towards a politicized movement. These political groups campaigned vociferously for land rights and social and economic equality. It seems that the first major breakthrough was in 1967 when the indigenous Australians were recognized as voting citizens and this led to subsequent successes in demands for land rights.

The Northern Territory has seen greater progress than many states on the issue of land rights. Nearly half the land is Aborigine-owned thanks to a 1976 Land Rights Act. Since then, in 1985, the Uluru National Park, which includes Ayers Rock, has been returned to the native Anangu. Much of the returned land, excluding the National Parks, is out of bounds to visitors without permits.

The land rights successes encouraged the Outstation Movement in the 1970s which resulted in Aborigines leaving the settlements and

An Aborigine playing the didgeridoo, wearing traditional gear and face paint. We filmed him for the opening sequence of the tv series.

Tiwi people on Bathurst Island. Their community is seen as a model for Aboriginal self-determination.

returning to a more traditional nomadic existence on their own land. The artist Jimmy Pike and many others returned to the Outback at this time. But what sort of a life were they returning to?

Surprisingly, maybe, many of these returning Aborigines looked to uphold the traditional beliefs. Social traditions include the men hunting for food, with the women rearing the children and implementing the various rituals and laws. But by the 1970s the backdrop against which these rituals are acted out had changed. For thousands of years the Aborigine tribes had lived in the desert. In their absence the Outback had altered: animals had disappeared and new predators had taken hold, and waterholes had silted up through neglect. The returning people were forced into re-interpreting the Aboriginal culture and lifestyle to re-establish their communities.

The increasing political clout of the Aborigine and their growing self-determination seems today to be going hand in hand with a renaissance in Aboriginal culture in these new communities. While this new self-expression can be seen in terms of the adaption of the

traditional lifestyle and spirituality, it's most evident in the field of arts and crafts.

This boom in native art over the last decade or so is not only of great economic importance to the Aborigine people – indeed income from this supports and gives economic freedom to a high proportion of Aboriginal communities – but the people are using the visual and performing arts to communicate their culture, spirituality and history to the non-Aboriginal population.

There is still great prejudice and misunderstanding on both sides to overcome. The most disappointing thing is that when you visit Australia, you see so few examples of Aboriginal people who have been successful. Most of those you see in the cities or on the road are poor and are often outcasts of their own Aboriginal communities, and this gives a misleading picture of who they actually are. I did see an Aboriginal man staying in my hotel in Darwin who was dresssed like a conventional businessman and it took me by surprise, which it shouldn't have done.

Tiwi artist at work. Their fabric designs are becoming famous all over the world.

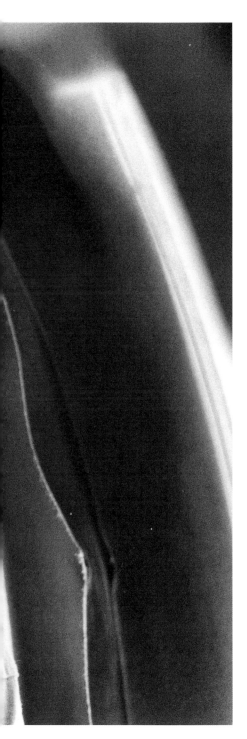

BATHURST ISLAND

One of the ways in which the Aboriginal people share their culture and lifestyle is by opening selected communities to outside visitors. Having fought for and won land rights, the Aborigines have quite rightly safeguarded these areas by closing them to visitors unless they carry the appropriate passes and permissions. This enables the Aboriginal communities to get on with their lives and to share their culture on their own terms, rather than just as some tourist sideshow. Permits are normally only given if you are visiting friends or relatives, or if you are going as part of an authorized tour. This gives the communities control over who will visit and when. In addition to this, the permit system is often waived for Aboriginal festivals on restricted land.

Whilst in Darwin I had the opportunity to visit the Bathurst and Melville Islands, collectively known as the Tiwi Islands – which are about 80 kilometres off the north coast. These two flat islands are home to the Tiwi Aborigines and are Australia's largest islands after Tasmania. The islands are owned by the Aborigines who run their own affairs and control the number of visitors.

The Tiwi's island homes kept them isolated from mainland developments for many years and their hostility to all invaders led to the premature failure of a British outpost on Melville Island just five years after it was established in 1824. A Belgian missionary set up a Catholic mission on Bathurst Island in 1911 on the site of the present town – Nguiu – and in the intervening years the Tiwi people have evolved from a hunter/gatherer lifestyle to a commodity-based economy reliant on clothing, pottery, screen printing and painting. And very happy they seem.

Clearly there is now a non-traditional lifestyle on Bathurst but many Tiwi go back to their traditional lands on Melville Island for a couple of weeks a year. Interestingly, and a little bizarrely, Melville Island is also home to the descendants of the Japanese pearl fishers who came there at the beginning of the century.

Now the Tiwi people claim quite a colourful heritage for themselves. They believe that they are all descended from an old blind woman called Mudangkala who is said to have emerged from the earth thousands and thousands of years ago carrying three babies. She crawled across the land, and where she had crawled the water followed her, making lakes, rivers and seas. She then put plants, animals and

On the plane to Bathurst Island.

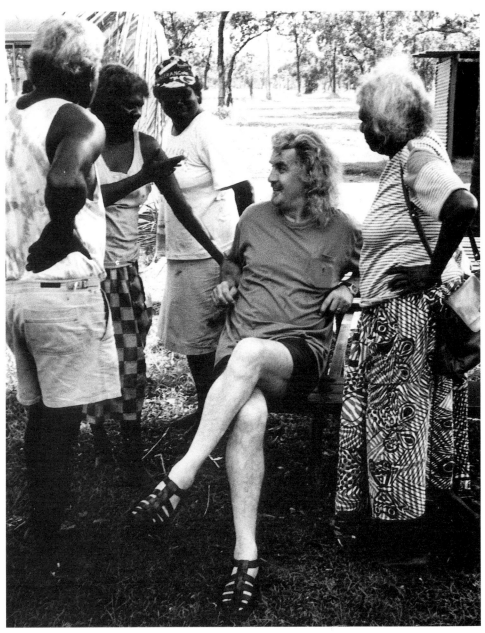

Above: I felt right at home among the Tiwi on the island, finding out about their history and their lives today.

Left: This is a great lady called Eleanor who took me crabbing for 'muddies'.

people on the land. The people descended from her are called the Imunga, and membership is passed through the mother. There is also a land-owning group, membership of which is passed through the father, who are called the Country People. Both peoples live in harmony and it seems that the Country People are more responsible for the affairs of the land, and the Imunga look after the more spiritual side – 'Dreaming' and so on.

> *Have you ever seen an ugly fish? It's very aptly named. It's got a big ugly head, like a wart, and a huge body with a little tail. The only edible bit of it is just before the tail – its arse. Imagine going through life being called an ugly fish and your best feature is your arse.*

Bathurst Island seems to be set up as some sort of model for Aboriginal cultural and economic self-determination. I think it's great. I really want to see these people winning, to see them living their lives in the way they want to, rather than seeing them unhappily tacked on to the end of somebody else's idea of civilization.

A unique feature of the Tiwi culture is the 'Pukumani' burial poles – carved and painted with mythological figures, and erected around graves. The Pukumani burial rites are one of the key rituals of Tiwi religious life and it is around these rites that some of the other art forms unique to Bathurst Island are created, including the bark baskets, spears and poles. The poles can be up to 2.5 metres long and are carved using ironwood. These artefacts, along with sculptures, birds and animals are the most traditional art forms of Bathurst.

The Tiwi also believe that there is a spirit living on the island called Mimi Mimi – and if you have trouble conceiving a child, you just come here with your wife, and Bingo!

Tiwi Food

I was given a delightful welcome on the beach by the Tiwi. And now, we're off in search of Bathurst's finest food. The Tiwi are self-sufficient and hunt for much of their food. On the beach we tracked down some mud crabs – 'muddies'. Believe me, you've never eaten until you've had a muddie – they're to die for. The Tiwi use a specially-fashioned stick to hook the crab's limbs and pull him out of the mud. The one we caught and ate was called a blue swimmer. The Tiwi use the pincers to make a pipe which the women particularly are very fond of smoking.

Next on the menu was a real delicacy: mangrove worm. The worms live in trees and the Tiwi go wild for them. They hack into the tree, pull out the worms and eat them alive! I suppose it's not very different from an oyster. I was dreading eating one but it wasn't so bad. They leave a taste in your mouth that lingers long after the event. It's a very fresh taste, a bit like the sea and a bit revolting really. But I've had worse things in my mouth. The previous time that I had eaten a worm was when I was in the Army, and then you just squeezed out the stuff in the middle and ate the casing only, for the protein they said.

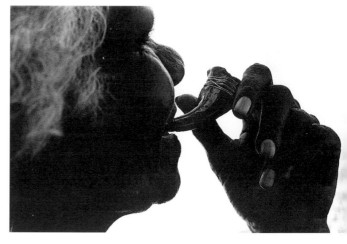

I was shown various leaves and plants which could be eaten, or used for dye, weaving or making soap. I was impressed with the green plums which tasted like ginger beer.

Next we made our way through the forest for a proper barbie: grilled frill-necked lizard and magpie goose. The goose is literally cut down the centre and laid, guts, feathers and all on the fire.

Above: Catch your muddie, then make a pipe from its pincers.

Below: On the beach with the expert catchers.

Tiwi Crafts Centre

After experiencing the new taste sensations, I decided that it was time to check out the Tiwi Design Centre, where they make all the crafts.

Despite the walls being corrugated iron, they look great. I mean, corrugated iron is useful but it doesn't always look good. Their colourful design looks wonderful.

Inside the centre the Tiwi were screen-printing silks, carving wood, making burial poles, painting and weaving. Everything is made by hand. The island is a true workers' co-operative, owned by the Tiwi. It's just like our hunting for food earlier, as everything is brought back and shared. It's really a pretty wonderful society and there's a lovely atmosphere on the island. We could learn a great deal from these people.

I particularly loved the paintings, which are very fine and traditional, and the burial poles, which are like gravestones except that they tell a much better story.

Above: The striking designs on the walls of the Tiwis' craft centre.

Opposite: 'Open your mouth Billy, here's your worm!'

❝Men always sleep holding their willy. There are very good reasons for it. It goes back to the dawn of time when cavemen lived in fear because testicle-eating wolves roamed the earth.❞

❝Who discovered that milk comes from cows? What do you think he thought he was doing at the time?❞

Isn't it funny how life changes? I used to be a welder from Glasgow. This isn't the poor but honest, from humble stock made good blarney – it's just the way it is. I used to be a welder and since I've become a comedian, my life has changed beyond all recognition. Just recently it came home to me how much it has altered. My seven-year-old daughter Amy came up and said to me 'Daddy, Mum says that if I don't learn my eight-times table I won't be going to Paris at the weekend.' In my day it was, 'If you don't do your eight-times table I'll kick your arse.' I pondered the mystery of life awhile and then said 'Shut up and eat your quiche, you pretentious little prick!'

I used to be obsessed with death, and spent all my time hanging around graveyards. Don't ask me why. It was the late 1960s. I was obsessed with death for a long time and now I'm not at all. If anything I'm obsessed with life. I'm constantly talking to people. I seem to have an approachable face. People even talk to me in toilets.

I had to go to the doctor for a medical. Is there anything worse than handing a jar of warm piss to an attractive woman?

I have reached a very happy stage in my life and, as a result, my work is getting better. Everything is improving. It's all working out nicely.

THAT'S ALL, FOLKS

Well, that's the end of a long and interesting journey. I've loved every second of it, and I hope you've enjoyed it as much as I have. I've seen places and people I haven't seen in a long long time and I've done some new and exciting things – such as going to the islands to see the Tiwi Aborigines, an experience which will remain with me all my life. It's been immensely enjoyable.

From the south where the temperature is rather like Britain, to the north where you only get two seasons – wet and dry, to the hot dry centre, I've tried to convey the mood of Australia – its incredible brightness and youthful vitality. If I've succeeded a little, I'll be happy.

It's been a real gas. Maybe we'll go somewhere else next time. See you again.

CREDITS

BBC Worldwide Publishing would like to thank the following for providing photographs and for permission to reproduce copyright material. While every effort has been made to trace and acknowledge all copyright holders, we would like to apologize should there have been any errors or omissions.

ART GALLERY OF NEW SOUTH WALES pages 37 Graham McCarter *Whiteley, Reiby Place, Sydney 1985*, & 39 Brett Whiteley *Lyrebird* 1972-3. Oil & mixed media on canvas 198 x 183.5 x 26 cm. Private Collection; ASSOCIATED PRESS page 77 *top right*; AUSCAPE INTERNATIONAL pages 63, 66-7, 91, 94-5, 114-15 *main picture*, 127 *top*, 130-1, 134, 144-5 *main picture*, 150-1, 162 & 163; AUSTRALIAN TOURIST COMMISSION pages 18 (Paul Kenwood), 35, 79 *left*, 120, 145 *inset*, 146-7 (Nick Rains) & 174-5; KEN DONE GALLERY pages 27 & 30; E.T. ARCHIVE pages 14-15; PIP GRANT-TAYLOR pages 21; THE HANCOCK MUSEUM pages 103; ROBERT HARDING PICTURE LIBRARY page 71; HULTON GETTY PICTURE COLLECTION pages 13 *bottom* & 75 *right*; LOCHMAN TRANSPARENCIES page 102 *top*; LYONS TETLEY AUSTRALIA LTD page 139; NATIONAL MARITIME MUSEUM, LONDON page 13 *top*; NATIONAL TRUST OF AUSTRALIA page 79 *inset right*; SLEEPY DUMPLING (MUSIC) LTD pages 25, 26 *bottom*, 29, 32 *left*, 34, 38, 47 *inset*, 78, 80 *bottom*, 86 *top*, 93, 94, 123 *bottom*, 127 *inset bottom*, 136, 138 & 156; STATE LIBRARY OF NEW SOUTH WALES page 52; STATE LIBRARY OF VICTORIA, LA TROBE COLLECTION pages 82 & 83; ZEFA pages 10-11, 20, 22-3, 42-3 *left*, 58-9, 118-9 & 142-3. The remaining photographs were specially taken by Nobby Clark.

The recipe on page 138 for making a Family Jewels Purse comes from *Rabbit on a Shovel* by Lummo, published by Primavera Press (Sydney 1993), and is reproduced by permission.

The following books were especially useful: Barry Pearce, *Brett Whiteley: Art & Life 1939-1992* (Thames & Hudson, 1995), *Ken Done: the art of design* (Powerhouse Publishing, 1994) and Peter Brady, *Whitefella Dreaming* (Preferred Image, 1994).